Miriam's Sisters,
Deborah's Daughters

Miriam's Sisters, Deborah's Daughters

When Women Lead the Way

Liz Crumlish

CANTERBURY
PRESS

© Liz Crumlish 2025

First published in 2025 by the Canterbury Press Norwich

Editorial office
3rd Floor, Invicta House
110 Golden Lane
London EC1Y 0TG, UK
www.canterburypress.co.uk

Canterbury Press is an imprint of Hymns Ancient & Modern Ltd
(a registered charity)

Hymns Ancient & Modern® is a registered trademark of
Hymns Ancient & Modern Ltd
13A Hellesdon Park Road, Norwich,
Norfolk NR6 5DR, UK

All rights reserved. No part of this publication may be reproduced,
stored in a retrieval system, or transmitted,
in any form or by any means, electronic, mechanical,
photocopying or otherwise, without the prior permission of
the publisher, Canterbury Press.

The Author has asserted her right under the Copyright, Designs and
Patents Act 1988 to be identified as the Author of this Work

Scripture quotations are from New Revised Standard Version Bible: Anglicized
Edition, copyright © 1989, 1995 National Council of the Churches of Christ in the
United States of America. Used by permission. All rights reserved worldwide.

British Library Cataloguing in Publication data

A catalogue record for this book is available
from the British Library

ISBN: 978 1 78622 605 1

EU GPSR Authorised Representative
LOGOS EUROPE, 9 rue Nicolas Poussin, 17000, LA ROCHELLE, France
E-mail: Contact@logoseurope.eu

Typeset by Regent Typesetting

Contents

Introduction: Leadership in Liminal Spaces   ix

   Transition poem   1
1. Leadership as Subversive   3
   Midwives poem   9
2. Leadership as Learning   11
   Miriam in Four Movements poem   17
3. Leadership as Calling it Out   19
   Showing Up poem   25
4. Leadership as Creating Peaceful Community   27
   Never Underestimate a Woman poem   33
5. Leadership as Resourcefulness   35
   Hospitality poem   39
6. Leadership as Orchestration   41
   Second Fiddle poem   47
7. Leadership as Survival   49
   Rizpah poem   55

8	Leadership as Turning Things Around	57
	Shrouds poem	63
9	Leadership as Resistance	65
	'No' is a Complete Sentence poem	71
10	Leadership as Prophetic	73
	Unholy Trinity poem	77
11	Leadership as Song	79
	God Bearers poem	87
12	Leadership as Tenacity	89
	Mary, Mother of God poem	93
13	Leadership as Making Poetry	95
	The Art of Contemplation poem	99
14	Leadership as Finding Our Voice	101
	A Woman Possessed poem	105
15	Leadership as Breaking the Mould	107
	Recovering Her Story poem	111
16	Leadership as Fostering Wellbeing	113
	Resonance poem	117
17	Leadership as Collaboration	119
	Women with Pockets in Their Dresses poem	123
18	Navigating by Old Landmarks	125
	Epitaph poem	127

References and Further Reading   129

For Idris,
who continues to love me
through every iteration of
who I am still becoming

Introduction: Leadership in Liminal Spaces

Keep some room in your heart for the unimaginable.
Mary Oliver (2010)

One of my favourite words is 'liminal', defined as a threshold, a space between.

My first adventure in full-time ordained ministry was in hospital chaplaincy, and liminal described perfectly the interface in which I mostly found myself working – encompassing faith and ritual, folk religion and superstition. It straddled the chasm that folk often felt when their experience of life and faith, if they professed faith, no longer accommodated their place when they found themselves caught up in the landscape of illness and loss – whether it was their own illness and loss or that of a loved one. That place where there were no easy answers – or any answers at all – where there was the sense of relinquishing one reality without being sure of what might take its place. My role was one of accompaniment through unfamiliar territory.

In stark contrast to that experience of journeying alongside, much of the leadership teaching and training I have received focuses on strategies, goals and outcomes. It consists of many acronyms, graphs, diagrams and bullet points. There is a persistent attempt to fit prescribed one-size-fits-all models onto messy realities. The desired outcome seems to be uniform change, often sought through conformity to a carefully laid-out programme that eliminates anomaly, disenfranchises choice and barely acknowledges the pain of loss that is an integral part of any kind of change.

As people of faith today, we are called to inhabit liminal spaces – those borderlands, those places of transition. They are the habitat of the people of God, places of learning and of transformation, places where grief and loss can be weathered together.

Before any change can be effected, transition is necessary, and that is a journey most effectively traversed with accompaniment, with support and by learning together, often through trial and error along the way. No amount of teaching or theorizing or cleverly crafted strategies can replace the commitment to walk alongside others as, together, we find a way through the changed landscape in which the Church seeks to be an effective witness to faith, hope and love today. Transition focuses not on the end goal, but on the winding path that intentionally makes space for the emotions to catch up so that we can fully inhabit whatever the new reality will look like. We navigate transition both individually and in community.

My premise is that in the stories of so many biblical women we find examples of what leadership looks like in liminal times, and in their stories there is a depth of wisdom to be gleaned as we seek to lead people through liminality today.

My contention is that the Church is tasked to live in constant liminality, always on the cusp of transitioning into something new. And strategies of leadership that seek to fix in place ways

INTRODUCTION: LEADERSHIP IN LIMINAL SPACES

of being defer the momentum of movement and risk inhibiting life and growth.

In every age, women have exchanged stories as they went about the business of everyday life. They shared ancient wisdom as they gathered around the well to draw water, as they went 'down to the river to pray' and in the myriad other places where women gathered and engaged in age-old practices that kept life together. Their stories forged connections and ensured that wisdom was shared between successive generations and between communities.

Part of my work involves leading retreats from time to time. Whatever the theme of the retreat, bringing groups together to hear one another's stories is the element that most often proves life giving. Human beings are storied beings. In listening to one another's stories, we find connections and forge relationships. In preserving stories, we keep alive traditions and community cultures that have shaped the present and will continue to shape the future. There is something in convincing people that their stories matter that feels like sacred work. To be re-storied is to be re-membered.

Where I live in Scotland, every community would have a Seanchaidh, a bearer of stories who passed on the rich history and tradition of a culture from generation to generation. Sometimes their art was downplayed as a good evening's entertainment, as they recounted tales that provoked mirth and fear in equal measure. But the reach and purpose of the Seanchaidh drilled much deeper, provoking insight and wisdom that transcended the passage of time, preserving the very root of the community's psyche. The Seanchaidh was able to incisively name what she saw, to call it out, alerting attention and leaving interpretation open. When any of us make space to hear one another's stories, remaining curious, without judgement, we begin to restore a sense of shared community and endeavour.

This book was conceived in the contemplation of the subversive practices of the Hebrew midwives, Shiphrah and Puah. It is not insignificant that just one of the areas of contemporary life in which we see women's stories subsumed is that of the practice of midwifery. In a healing art concerned with assisting the body's natural processes, an art in which women have engaged intuitively and experientially since time began, scientific rigour and medical efficiency rely heavily on the oral and practical tradition of women's ways of knowing. We would be foolish to exchange protocols for intuitive wisdom and replace sense-making stories with analytical pathways.

In one of the Gospel stories, in John 4, the woman who encountered Jesus at the well carried with her, in that encounter, generations of those who had gone before her. Her wisdom met divine wisdom and in that meeting was transformation, for the woman, for Jesus and, subsequently, for a whole community as they followed the woman to the well to see for themselves the source of the water of life. Photini, as she became known, is just one of Miriam's sisters and Deborah's daughters.

You are invited to enter the stories of other biblical women as they emerge from the confines of patriarchy to shed light on how we might lead the people of God today, living in liminal spaces and finding transformation in transition.

Transition

Described as the space between trapezes
Not possible without a letting go
Difficult enough when it is chosen
Even harder when imposed
When we find ourselves suspended
in that space between
who will encourage us onward
to continue on the arc
that may take us further than we have ever gone before?
And if that time
of being suspended in mid-air
is longer than anticipated
who will risk
stepping into the void alongside us?
Who will join us
in that wild and precarious space
that speaks of possibility
that invites creativity
that is pregnant with potential?
Who will hear our story
help us re-member
and commit
to the next part of the journey
as we reach for a touching point
that remembers what was
celebrates what is
and transforms what will be?

1

Leadership as Subversive

The sight of women talking together has always made men uneasy; nowadays it means rank subversion.
Germaine Greer (2020)

I was a mature student by the time I went to study theology. I was cautioned by many of my spiritual mentors at the time that pursuing theology at a 'secular' university would try my faith in ways I had never encountered. That much was true – but not in the ways my friends had feared or predicted. I revelled in the endeavour of dismantling the story I thought I knew to try and piece it together in a very different way – a pursuit that remains a lifelong engagement and commitment. The constructs of faith still feel, for me, like a giant tower of wooden blocks, precarious in its formation, just waiting to be toppled. And that toppling is accompanied by raucous laughter and an easy commitment to begin construction all over again. I love to be reminded, when I've settled for some kind of stability, of the shaky nature of building blocks that are riddled with all the flaws of human constructs and attempts to control a narrative that is wild and free and timeless, the narrative of God.

This realization, that faith consists in continually dismantling and piecing together capricious constructs, came home to roost, alarmingly, one weekend, when I was asked to preach on the story of Moses encountering the burning bush in the desert. Working for an institution whose emblem is the burning bush, encircled by the words *nec tamen consumebatur*, I had never before troubled to question that motif and those words, instead readily accepting them as some of the foundational symbols of faith. But as I sought to locate Moses in a wider narrative of the journey of the people of God, I was struck by something of the ridiculous in that desert encounter. Although I did, that weekend, preach a tongue-in-cheek sermon about a God who hides in bushes and calls out wimps, it would be some time before I returned to locating more fiercely my discomfort with the overarching Moses story as portrayed in an era that was still being shaped by the icon that was Charlton Heston in the 1956 film, *The Ten Commandments*.

So began a wild and exhilarating roller coaster ride.

It was in the first stages of that journey that I encountered the Hebrew midwives, Shiphrah and Puah, and in the account of their subversiveness I felt seen.

Shiphrah and Puah, who attended Jochebed, mother of Miriam, might have confronted Pharaoh when he issued the decree that all male children should be killed at birth. That way would surely have led to their disappearance. However, they recognized that they could do more good by simply going about their work and allowing the ingenuity of other women to save the lives of their sons. When they were called to account for their actions, or lack thereof, they spoke the truth and Pharaoh was confronted by just one of the flaws in his plan to exert absolute rule by infanticide: the ingenuity of women.

Those midwives became role models for me, a sign of hope, growing up in the midst of patriarchal oppression and disempowerment.

LEADERSHIP AS SUBVERSIVE

Shiphrah and Puah were among the first biblical women who inspired me to consciously cultivate subversive practice.

It wasn't that I hadn't been practising subversion.

I was born a twin – 30 minutes before my brother who was very sickly at birth. From an early age, I learned to be strong enough for both of us. I became his spokesperson. When my brother spoke, folk would look to me for an interpretation. And, perhaps because I was speaking for two, I learned economy with words. It's an economy that plays out today in my reluctance to fight for my voice to be heard in a room full of, usually male, colleagues. My philosophy, when told that something was not possible, has long been – just watch! (Or hold my beer!) Why waste words disputing when actions speak so much louder? Subversion had already become second nature to me.

Early on, I learned the efficacy of subversion. When confrontation became too painful and futile, I realized that subversion often achieved the intended outcome without the heartache.

Still today, when I am advised that a creative solution will not work, I will smile, move on and, more often than not, try it anyway – learning more from failure, should that be the outcome, than from not having tried. Life consists of learning how to use mishaps to shape the future. There are always those who will tread on our dreams. Finding imaginative ways to keep those dreams alive becomes imperative.

The story of those Hebrew midwives somehow legitimized for me the subversion in which I was already engaged.

My own experience of midwives before, during and after the process of giving birth is one of advocacy and empowerment. It is said that the uterus is the strongest muscle, by weight, in the body. Its many layers, running in different directions, orchestrate phenomenal pressure to give birth to a baby. It is hardly surprising then that men have in every age sought to exert power over the uterus in order to maintain patriarchal dominance by denying women the right to exercise control over their bodies and, in particular, over their reproductive choices.

The midwives with whom I was fortunate to have relationships had learned to be subversive, displaying courage in the face of imperial pronouncements that did not put the needs of mothers and babies front and centre. I encountered women who were prepared to confront those men involved in obstetrics or paediatrics who sometimes sought efficiency and expediency over listening to the wisdom and instinct of mothers.

The story of the Exodus of the people of God is a story too often told through patriarchal narrative when, from its very origins, it is women who are pivotal in its unfolding.

Shiphrah and *Puah*, the midwives who, rather than confront Pharaoh about his genocide, simply went about their business of ushering in new life.

Jochebed, who birthed Moses, nursed him and collaborated in an elaborate plan to preserve his life.

Miriam, the sister who executed that plan by watching over her brother and transacted an arrangement with *Bithiah*, the daughter of Pharaoh who took Moses, once weaned, back to the palace to be raised with standing and privilege.

All of these women birthed the Exodus. They did so by harnessing natural rhythms and working together.

I grew to recognize that the symbol with which I wanted to journey was not that of the burning bush (important as that has become for me) but that of the birthing stool – a constant reminder that there are many ways of finding and serving God in everyday life and work but that it all begins in the messiness of birth. And surely if there is one place that a woman should be

LEADERSHIP AS SUBVERSIVE

afforded the courtesy of being in charge, it is in the act of giving birth. Traditional birthing stools allow a woman to manage the birthing process while upright, rather than being confined in a medicalized horizontal position as is often the way. Some of the more modern versions of the birthing stool, birthing balls or birthing pools, similarly afford a woman some control over her delivery.

Midwifery from its earliest days has thrived on narrative, on listening carefully to women's stories and experience and finding ways to formulate good practice by observation, by facilitation and by enabling women to take control, as far as possible, of a natural process. This results, not in a neat, medicalized pathway, but in a messy and often unpredictable journey that is rhythmically attuned to the breath of creation.

I can only imagine how the image of a birthing stool would be received in our religious institutions, and yet the process of birth is something we have all experienced. We have, all of us, journeyed through the broken waters of a woman to begin our journey into life. The symbolism of birth is very apposite to the journey of faith.

None of us would deny that the Church finds itself in a dramatically altered landscape. To thrive in such a terrain means that we have to sift through the things of our past, retain or reclaim what is still useful in our new environment, jettison those things that hold us back, and find new solutions and new methods of engagement with our culture today, some of which may be ancient practices and symbols.

In an era that calls for adaptive leadership, finding imaginative and creative ways around obstacles is useful in the challenges that confront us today, where the technical expertise that many systems have relied on for so long no longer cuts the mustard in an age of change. When 'problems' can no longer be solved with the tools readily at hand, it's time to experiment with new things that allow us to engage with a new culture. This is not about survival but about thriving in a changed and changing environment.

That calls for leaders who are fuelled and sustained by prayer, Scripture and sacraments, and are willing not to look for a quick fix but to try out new ways of engagement, new ways of being Church today. Leaders who are able to hold their nerve and not resort to grasping hold of the latest programme or acronym or even the latest trend, but who recognize these as temporary fixes that won't build the resilience that being involved in the mission of God demands of us today. It's time not to ditch the DNA of the Church, but to be involved in its transformation so that it will thrive and be strengthened for today. Women have proved themselves adept in this kind of ingenuity, having been forced to develop the necessary skills to subvert patriarchal norms that stifle creative endeavour, and to chart new paths that honour timeless ways. Ditching the burning bush for the birthing stool may be a step too far for some, but it is perhaps a more honest and realistic symbol of the birth and rebirth that is required for the Church as an institution to survive.

Midwives

The ones who stand in the abyss
between life and death
easing life in, keeping death out
The ones who possess gifts of calm reassurance
along with skills of labouring to get the hard work done
The ones who know the liminality of birth
standing on a threshold that holds promise and fear
The ones who revere the strength and power of the uterus
to do what needs to be done
The ones who, time and again,
bear witness to the emergence of new life
through the broken waters of women
The ones whose hands are the first to greet that new life
and shake it into being
grasping potential and giving it form
The ones who recognize in the sacredness of their task
their calling to stand for a time in the breach
before letting go and moving on
to ease another's labour
and greet the wonder and miracle of birth

2

Leadership as Learning

Do the best you can until you know better.
Then when you know better, do better.
Maya Angelou (in conversation)

Daughter, sister, leader, prophet – at every age it seems Miriam demonstrated her versatility, her power and her vulnerability. Always willing to show up, she effected change for herself and for her brothers and sisters on the journey through the wilderness. She was the one who led the women in a song and a dance to celebrate their escape from Egypt. She was the one without whom the whole camp refused to move on when she was temporarily exiled.

Miriam is one of only a handful of women who are named as prophets in the biblical narrative. As well as featuring in the stories of Exodus, Miriam is named alongside her brothers Moses and Aaron by the prophet Micah (6.4–8) as he exhorts the people to remember their God and to do what God requires: 'to do justice, to love kindness and to walk humbly with God'.

There's a curious story about Miriam in Numbers 12, when it seems Miriam is punished after speaking out against Moses.

> While they were at Hazeroth, Miriam and Aaron spoke against Moses because of the Cushite woman whom he had married (for he had indeed married a Cushite woman); and they said, 'Has the Lord spoken only through Moses? Has he not spoken through us also?' (Num. 12.1–2)

There are a number of ways in which this text has been interpreted.

The Revd Dr Wil Gafney speaks of Miriam's 'sin' as that of speaking about her brother rather than to him (2012). This interpretation is a great reminder that more harm than good comes from speaking behind someone's back rather than confronting them directly.

Rabbi Danya Ruttenberg suggests that Miriam was shut out of the camp for asking awkward questions (2024), providing another endlessly intriguing possibility as we see increasingly today a surge in the silencing of women who speak out or who draw attention to those voices that are not being included in important conversations.

Whatever the interpretation, of note is the fact that there is no mention of Aaron being censured for his part in the incident. And perhaps more significantly, when Miriam is shut out of the camp for seven days, the people refused to move on without her. The people showed their loyalty and perhaps their disdain of her treatment by sticking around until she was readmitted and able to continue the journey with them.

Whatever the detail that we are unable to extract from the narrative at this juncture in history to help us see the whole picture, what seems clear is that Miriam was willing to show up and to speak up. And then she was willing to accept the consequences of being a persistent irritant.

Kristen Visbal created the sculpture that became known as the 'Fearless Girl', which was placed in Wall Street to commemorate International Women's Day 2017. Its juxtaposition with the 'Charging Bull' sculpture made a powerful statement on women's empowerment. It has since been moved to the New York Stock Exchange and continues to stand as a symbol of gender discrimination in places of power. In September 2020, the artwork was adorned with a lace collar in tribute to Justice Ruth Bader Ginsburg, who once said: 'Women belong in all places where decisions are being made.' Decorating the Fearless Girl sculpture with one of her signature lace collars recognized and celebrated Bader Ginsburg's legacy of speaking truth to power and of continuing to run the gauntlet of patriarchal bullshit.

'Nevertheless she persisted' has become a by-line for women who refuse to be silenced. It was a phrase coined in the wake of the rebuke and attempted silencing of Senator Elizabeth Warren in 2017 when she attempted to speak against the confirmation of the US attorney general. Despite the silencing, her speech went viral and attracted much more attention than it might otherwise have done if she'd simply been allowed to speak uninterrupted in the first place.

How are we to notice and amplify the missing voices in public debate today, and how might we resist speaking up for those whose voices are not being heard but rather agitate and advocate for their right to speak for themselves?

Whatever the interpretation of the heavily redacted passage in Numbers 12, what is clear is that once Miriam had done her time, she came back stronger. She returned to the fray, carrying all that she learned, for good or ill, and took her place again to effect change. With many wounds to lick, in the midst of disappointment and disillusionment, it would be easy to stay out of the spotlight rather than get back in it. Leadership calls for us to continue to show up. Therein lies both power and vulnerability, natural bedfellows in adversity and in change-making.

I am a fan of the drama series *Grey's Anatomy*. From my frequent sojourns into the escapism it provides, I have learned from some great and empowering techniques that are played out in the medical drama.

In one episode, just before a crucial surgery, Dr Stephanie Edwards walks into the scrub room and finds Dr Amelia Shepherd, her surgeon colleague, standing with her hands on her hips, chest stuck out and chin pointing upwards. On enquiring what's happening, Amelia tells her she is being a super-hero. Amelia claims, 'There's a scientific study that shows that if you stand like this in super-hero pose for just five minutes before a job interview or a big presentation or a really hard task, you will not only feel more confident, you will perform immeasurably better.' It's a great part in the drama – and becomes a refrain, played out at other points in the series. But it is also based on fact according to a 2012 Harvard study. From experience, I can confirm that the act of taking up a deliberate stance, breathing deeply and claiming space, does in fact enable calmness and confidence.

Another recurrent theme in the series is the practice of 'dancing it out' when times get particularly stressful. This consists of blasting out some tunes and cutting some moves, another effective strategy in releasing tension and clearing some space for further engagement. An important part in learning in leadership is cultivating techniques that enable us to decompress. For Miriam, dancing and drumming were part of her healthy recovery, while *Grey's Anatomy* is part of mine.

LEADERSHIP AS LEARNING

From the annals of *Grey's*, the Fearless Girl of the New York Stock Exchange and the story of Miriam the prophet, who knew that the four movements of leadership might be: hovering, dancing, waiting, persisting? Seemingly innocuous poses that pack quite the punch in skilful leadership.

Miriam in Four Movements

Miriam hovered
and ensured the welfare of her baby brother
negotiating safe passage with Pharaoh's daughter
ensuring that the boy had every advantage in life
not least survival
Miriam danced
and led her sisters in celebrating their freedom
in their exodus from Egypt
wielding instrument and song
in a celebration of life
Miriam waited
when she was exiled
for asking awkward questions
and then resumed her place
as a leader and prophet
who sometimes got in the way
of a patriarchal agenda
Miriam persisted
in the task of ensuring
that those who were silenced
could be heard in the cacophony
of the male voice choir
that often drowned out
the voices of sisters
who reasoned with wisdom
Hovering, dancing, waiting, persisting
those well-known tasks of women
in every age and culture

3

Leadership as Calling it Out

They'll tell you you're too loud, that you need to wait your turn and ask the right people for permission. Do it anyway.
Alexandria Ocasio-Cortez (public address)

Mahlah, Noah, Hoglah, Milcah and Tirzah, known as the 'daughters of Zelophehad', challenged Moses about inheritance laws. Their father died leaving five daughters and no sons. As things then stood, women could not inherit, so Mahlah, Noah, Hoglah, Milcah and Tirzah petitioned Moses to be allowed to inherit their father's land. They were required to appear before Moses and the priest Eleazar, and all the chiefs gathered at the Tent of Meeting. After hearing from the women, Moses consulted God about their plea and discerned that the law should be changed. As is often the case when concessions are made, there was some clawback, and the amended law was later further modified. As the concession was implemented and the implications of women inheriting land became clearer, the law was amended to say that, although female relatives could inherit the land they must, when marrying, be yoked with someone within their own tribe so that the land would not be lost to foreigners. Nonetheless the willingness of these sisters to become visible changed the law and changed the lives of countless others.

Women are used to having to 'argue their case' before panels of men who may often be far less qualified or experienced than they are.

The annals of Scripture are littered with stories of women who, at great personal risk, emerged from the shadows, allowed themselves to be seen, and improved life for themselves and for others.

Contemporary history also conceals stories of women who made a difference, often receiving no recognition for their achievements.

Hidden Figures, a biography by Margot Lee Shetterly (2016), tells the story of the African-American women who worked at NASA, and as mathematicians contributed significantly to the space race. The film adaptation of the book dramatizes the story of three of those women, Katherine Goble Johnson, Dorothy Vaughan and Mary Jackson. It is perhaps inevitable that, in dramatizations, stories become different and characters become conflated; nevertheless we are afforded insight into these three women, and those they worked with, who were trailblazers, paving the way for some movement towards equality and progress.

Throughout history, there have always been women who have found a way to overcome patriarchy. Often their work goes largely unnoticed. Occasionally it is amplified as part of a larger campaign for equality.

While the world remembers Rosa Parks and her activism against segregation laws, few are aware of other activists like Claudette Colvin who, at the age of fifteen, was arrested for refusing to give up her seat on a bus. Although Claudette's protest took place a good nine months before Rosa Parks's, her young age was deemed too risky by activist organizations who wanted to orchestrate a more concerted effort and champion the actions of someone like Rosa Parks with whom more folk would identify.

In the UK, Emmeline Pankhurst is remembered for founding the Women's Social and Political Union in 1903 to organize robust and militant action in the fight for votes for women. Less well remembered is Millicent Fawcett who formed the National Union of Women's Suffrage Societies in 1897 to lobby peacefully for the parliamentary vote.

There is no doubt that all of these women played vital roles in leadership and in changes that many of us today take for granted. We keep their stories alive not simply to honour them, but to avoid slipping back into comfortable ways that allow those in power to subtly undermine stories that matter and erode hard-won victories. Who will keep faith with their stories?

Complacency runs the danger of colluding with those who seek to exploit false narratives.

Arguably, one of the most exploited stories is the story of the woman in the Garden of Eden.

> Now the serpent was more crafty than any other wild animal that the Lord God had made. He said to the woman, 'Did God say ...' (Gen. 3.1)

We know well how that story has been used as a way to speak of sin, of weakness and of a woman being the cause of the downfall of humankind. St Augustine has a lot to answer for. The doctrine of original sin that he overlaid on the garden story, and which was adopted by the Council of Trent in the sixteenth century, is one that has survived centuries of retelling.

This overlay is not one that is supported by the text. In the text, we discover that an unnamed woman listened to a clever serpent and weighed up the information she already had, along with the information that the serpent provided. The woman chose to avail herself of good food and so began a new chapter in her life, a chapter that consisted of living beyond the confines of the garden. And it is in that new life that she is eventually named as 'Eve, mother of all living' (Gen. 3.20).

This is all a long way from the narrative that is widely held and trotted out to support all kinds of injustice against womankind.

The denomination I served has been ordaining women since 1968 and there is an assumption at large that that makes it inclusive. However, there is much discrepancy between what is espoused and what is operant, demonstrated in the places where decisions are made within the denomination which are not at all representative or inclusive. It is a denomination that does not allow the possibility of 'opting out' of women's ordination as some others do. However, when women reach a place where exerting influence might be possible, they either find the culture too combative and difficult or, perhaps even worse, they settle in, with their feet under the table, and do not hold space for sisters who might join them. Herstory is quickly forgotten, even by those whose story it is.

The courage that Mahlah, Noah, Hoglah, Milcah and Tirzah displayed was something that they had to revisit time and again. As is often the way, decrees do not become actions without activists continuing to show up and serve reminders. When others in their tribe wondered what would happen when the sisters married, they had to agree to marry within the tribe to preserve their rights. And, when it was finally time to enter the promised land under the leadership of Joshua, since Moses had died, they had to speak up again to ensure they received their allotted portion of land because Moses, despite consulting God and relaying God's decree, had failed to act. Isn't it peculiar that Moses, whose existence began with the intervention of five women – Jochebed, Shiphrah, Puah, Miriam and Bithiah – went to his grave having failed to enact justice for another five women, Mahlah, Noah, Hoglah, Milcah and Tirzah? What curious symmetry.

Mahlah, Noah, Hoglah, Milcah and Tirzah showed up and continued to show up, not just for themselves, but for all who came after. They persisted until what was promised was enacted. Only by remembering her story can we avoid repeating it.

Showing Up

in a room full of men
Men who have authority
Men who have power
always takes courage
no matter how much we practice
Because our muscle memory reminds us
of past experience in a hostile arena
Mahlah
Noah
Hoglah
Milcah
Tirzah
were women
who knew their vulnerability
and who stepped into their power
Leaving the place assigned them
they entered the place where decisions were made
Armed with truth
they confronted the law
and the patriarchy
They pleaded their case
were heard
and achieved change
for themselves
and for the women who followed
Not only did they confront power
with knowledge and truth

MIRIAM'S SISTERS, DEBORAH'S DAUGHTERS

they also held space
and kept on showing up
for their sisters of the future
Victory is hollow
short-lived
unless it leads to
lasting change
Called to be courageous
Called to transform vulnerability into power
Called to model sisterhood
By showing up to confront patriarchy
in all its guises today

4

Leadership as Creating Peaceful Community

I am a woman and a warrior. If you think I can't be both, you've been lied to.
Jennifer Zeynab Joukhadar (2019)

Because of her, the land had rest for forty years.
Judges 3.11

What an epitaph. In the midst of tribal turf wars, lawlessness and violence, Deborah, as judge and prophet, brought an extensive period of calm. Perhaps she was that non-anxious presence that is promoted as an aspiration for leaders today. It's not that Deborah did not go to war. Rather that by the time she did, she had done a lot of behind-the-scenes hard work. As a result of her efforts in building community, Deborah commanded a unified force and chose her battles carefully. Deborah was a collaborative leader. She inherited not just a single community but a series of disparate tribes, enemies and allies, who were still learning hard lessons in sharing land and in living cheek by jowl. Deborah was there for that learning.

Deborah discerned the guidance of YHWH and enlisted appropriate support to create some kind of peace and community where lots of different factions were actively learning how to live together and how to create peaceful community. Deborah knew the value of tending to her immediate surroundings, finding commonalities, so that when she brought her warriors together under one umbrella to tackle an opposing force, she had already earned their trust and allegiance, along with the recognition that she was YHWH's emissary.

There is no real evidence that Deborah was married. 'Lappidoth' referred to in the text is more likely to be a description of Deborah as 'fiery' rather than the name of her partner. And yet she is called a 'mother in Israel'. That epithet, just as surely as her accolades as warrior, judge, prophet or intermediary, was a title of great honour. She rose as a mother in Israel to fight with all the passion of a mother with and for her people. She showed her 'offspring' how to play nicely with one another and led them in battle when necessary. She bequeathed a great legacy of tough mother love for all who followed.

Deborah did not subscribe to any formulaic approach to leadership. She dwelled among the people, heard their stories and imbued their culture, of which she was a part. She listened to God's spirit of guidance within her and encouraged the people to work alongside her in writing the next chapter of their life together – both her story and history.

Deborah's song in Judges 5, probably one of the oldest parts of Hebrew Scripture, is a song shared with Barak. It commemorates their victory together with all the people, and remains a worthy testament to a judge, prophet, mother, peacemaker, warrior and leader who emerged as one of her people.

Those who emerge as leaders from within cultures, as part of the storied landscape, have the potential to be real influencers among their contemporaries. Sometimes, however, there is work to be done in overcoming what is known as 'tall poppy' syndrome, people criticizing those who are successful. And indeed there are ways of using such diminishment, designed to help folks know their place, for the good of all. When someone takes the trouble to remind us of our origins it can be both a source of pride and a caution. We can embrace our humble beginnings to amplify potential as well as to ground ourselves in current reality by acknowledging the various ways that our community has contributed to our development. We often see the folks around Jesus questioning his authority by muttering about his heritage:

> They were saying, 'Is not this Jesus, the son of Joseph, whose father and mother we know?' (John 6.42)

As I write, there's a ship being launched today from one of the Lower Clyde shipyards. It's likely to be the last of these kinds of affairs in a business that sees little work these days.

I was once chaplain in that shipyard simply because it sat in the parish I served, and in Scotland there was a tradition, now diminishing, of parish clergy providing workplace chaplaincy within parochial boundaries. As yard chaplain, I was welcomed into the life and work of the men in the yard. The only women on the workforce at that time were in the administration offices, or occasionally French polishers and seamstresses who were brought in to finish and to dress the ship's woodwork towards the end of the contract. As chaplain, I would call into the yard early in the morning, gathering with the men around an old oil drum in which the men lit a fire and over which they heated water. I learned to drink tea out of mugs without looking too closely at the cleanliness of the vessels, or indeed the captions that decorated the mugs. I listened as they told me with pride of the latest build in which they were involved and sometimes I was invited and encouraged to clamber aboard hulls of ships not yet named. I was fascinated by how great sheets of metal were rolled and shaped and welded together to form structure. My father had worked as a plater in a yard just a bit further down the river. And now, some 30 years on, equipped with a hard hat and steel-toe-capped boots, I was allowed to wander through these new ships being built. Although safety regulations were observed meticulously, I could see what a potentially hazardous occupation ship building could be. As a five-year-old, I remember my father recovering at home with two broken ankles, injuries sustained when he fell down one of the holds on a ship. As children, we had no awareness of the serious nature of his injuries that left our father with a permanent limp but simply enjoyed racing dad, whose legs were both in plaster cast, up and down the stairs in our home.

After several months of sharing in the early morning banter, I became the 'go to' pastor for those men as they marked births, deaths and marriages in their family lives. Although they 'kent [knew] my faither', or perhaps even because of that, I had become one of them, trusted to officiate at significant moments in their lives.

Just one of the more public community moments I shared with the workforce was the launch of a vessel for the Scottish Northern Lighthouse Board. Her Majesty Queen Elizabeth II was attending to launch the ship and I was invited to bless the ship immediately before Her Majesty named her. As I made my way up onto the platform with lots of dignitaries, a voice from the midst of the workers called out: 'Keep it short, hen!' An admonishment I understood only too well. Just the week before, the men had been describing the launch process to me, making sure I understood that because everything was well greased and ready to go ahead of the launch, if the ceremony went on too long, it could have dire consequences. That last-minute reminder certainly pricked any pomposity I may have felt as I stepped up to do my part.

Sometimes leadership looks like sitting, as Deborah did under a tree, where people knew they would find her, sharing wisdom and stories. Sometimes it looks like bringing communities together to notice what they have in common and to celebrate difference. And sometimes it looks like inciting communities to resist forces that threaten their existence, marking significant rites of passage along the way and celebrating victories large and small. In every instance, leadership looks like listening carefully to those we lead and pooling our resources to chart a future together.

There's a kind of postscript to Deborah's military leadership in the story of Jael. The leader of the Canaanite army, Sisera managed to escape the flooded field of battle, abandoning his troops. He sought refuge in the tent of Jael but, in doing so, he committed the fatal error of underestimating a woman. Jael showed him hospitality and then, when he fell asleep, she drove a tent peg through his skull. Meanwhile, Sisera's mother hovered by her window, anticipating the return of her son with the spoils of war. Deborah led her people into battle and Jael dispatched the commander of the opposing force and the people had rest for forty years.

Never Underestimate a Woman

As if his crimes were not heinous enough
As if deserting his command
and abandoning his troops
did not render him beyond the pale
Sisera made a fatal mistake
He underestimated a woman
A woman who was resourceful
Who was fearless
Who had tools to hand
A woman who bided her time
And served up revenge
Lukewarm rather than cold
A clean blow to the head ensured
He would never again
underestimate a woman
And all the while a mother awaited her son's return

5

Leadership as Resourcefulness

A refugee is someone who survived and who can create the future.
Amela Koluder (2021)

When I hear the story of Ruth, Naomi and Orpah against the backdrop of so many displaced people in the world today, just one of the things I wonder is how they decided what to take with them as they travelled across country. Like the countless refugees we see today, moving across borders, taking risks that they calculate are preferable to staying put, what becomes important enough to carry with them, if indeed there is opportunity to carry anything?

I'm reminded of a simulation that I often led when involved in training days for multi-disciplinary palliative care teams. Each participant would start with a limited number of cards on which they were invited to write the names of the people, places and objects that they perceived as their most valued, those things that added quality to their lives. The simulation proceeded with some of the cards being arbitrarily removed by others in the group, after which participants were asked to re-evaluate the things that were left. Often, although someone was left with one of their favourite places, or a favourite food, the important people with whom they wanted to share that would be missing. Life-limiting conditions do not respect our preferences. Similarly, those forced to flee their homes and countries are rarely free to make choices that enhance their quality of life.

Naomi was seasoned in making those kinds of choices, having fled her home to escape a famine. But when she undertook the outward journey, she did so in the company of her husband and two sons. Now it's time to reverse the direction and return to her home that has emerged from famine, to be with her own kith and kin, to wallow in her widowhood and to mourn the loss of her sons. Leaving that place that had brought such sorrow, what would matter enough to carry with her? Perhaps the dead weight of Naomi's shame and bitterness left little room for anything else.

Probably the last thing Naomi needed as baggage was an alien daughter-in-law, and a childless one at that, to attach herself to her misery. Isolation probably seemed preferable by far as she slunk back to her former home. Was she grateful to Orpah when she chose to return to her own kin? Perhaps Naomi, in her grief, did not see Ruth's determination to stay with her as something to be welcomed or applauded. Surely it amplified Naomi's failure as a matriarch in a culture where progeny was everything. Yet, together, Ruth and Naomi became a formidable force. Exploiting to the full the culture of hospitality and the levirate obligation of honouring the names of the dead, Ruth was suitably matched and bore Naomi the grandson she so desperately wanted. Then Naomi's arms were, once again, filled with love and with pride.

I admire Ruth's tenacity in sticking with her mother-in-law when she clearly wasn't wanted or when she was offered a clear escape route, and I wonder too how it might have felt for Ruth to contemplate returning to her own folks. Would she have been welcomed or would she have been seen as some kind of failure? Whatever Ruth's motive for staying, her selflessness did not stop at remaining with the embittered Naomi. When Ruth's first child was born, she surrendered him to Naomi, allowing Naomi to be the envy of her friends as she basked in the joy of Ruth's child.

The story of Ruth may well be a myth concocted to contribute to the clarity of Jesus' lineage, through Ruth/Naomi's son Obed to David, and it may have been placed where it is in the Canon to bring some welcome relief to the horror tales of Judges. It also contains not-so-veiled allusions to sexual manipulation in Ruth's alliance with Boaz. I continue to wonder, however, whether the kind of forced choices that Ruth made, choosing the least of several evils, remains the experience of refugees today who, with few resources and few options, all with the potential for danger, make the best decisions that they can in a world where chance is stacked against them. We concoct policies that make things even more difficult in an already impossible landscape in which we are quick to exile anyone who is 'not like us'. How might our lives be enriched and expanded if instead we allowed their stories to inform our policies?

Hospitality

Taking down the good china
a mismatched assortment
of colours and styles
once coveted and cherished
kept for high days and holy days
handled with reverence and care
Now remnants that continue to grace the table
carrying within them memories
and so many stories
of times of laughter and of tears
homecomings and reunions
funeral wakes and valedictories
new jobs and graduations
weddings and baptisms
retirals and deaths
And, like those who have handled these elements
through years of service
longtime friends and family
and friends not yet made
these vessels bear signs of wear
patterns have faded
chipped pieces discarded
or repurposed for plants and candles
Some missing pieces have been augmented
by different styles and patterns
adding vibrancy and colour
removing some of the formality

MIRIAM'S SISTERS, DEBORAH'S DAUGHTERS

of custom and tradition
Still, they are laid out with care
signalling a welcome
for the invited and the uninvited
who will find a place
at this table

6

Leadership as Orchestration

I can promise you that women working together – linked, informed and educated – can bring peace and prosperity to this forsaken planet.
Isabelle Allende (in conversation)

Often at the start of a new calendar year, or perhaps at the start of a new term, or a new liturgical season, church congregations will embark on Bible reading programmes. Some of these programmes aim to encourage reading through certain genres of Scripture, familiar and less familiar, or perhaps even a whole year of reading through the Old and New Testaments. Of course, there are some parts that are easier to stick with than others.

Reading through all the statistics of Numbers takes some commitment, as does reading through all the prescriptions of Leviticus. As stated elsewhere, the Book of Judges is particularly bloody and violent. But probably the most skipped-over passages in Scripture are the genealogies, those passages that begin X was the father of Y and Y was the father of Z … Or, as it is in other versions, X begat Y who begat Z … and on it goes. One such passage is in the first chapter of the Gospel of Matthew, where the Gospel writer recounts the genealogy of Jesus, 42 generations from which came the Messiah. In that genealogy, four women are mentioned in addition to Mary, mother of Jesus, although only three are mentioned by name. These are Tamar, Rahab, Ruth and 'the wife of Uriah' who is Bathsheba (the writer cannot bring himself to mention her name). The story of each of these women is a tale of ingenuity, resourcefulness and resilience and their inclusion in the genealogy is testament to that.

Tamar was the daughter-in-law of Judah twice over – she married one of Judah's sons, Er, and when he was killed she married his brother, Onan, as was the levirate custom that ensured that a family line might continue. However, despite the intention of levirate marriage to provide an heir, Onan made sure that Tamar didn't conceive, and he too was killed. Judah decided that Tamar must be cursed, so he was reluctant to give his third son, Shelah, to Tamar and claimed that he was too young.

> Then Judah said to his daughter-in-law Tamar, 'Remain a widow in your father's house until my son Shelah grows up' – for he feared that he too would die, like his brothers. So Tamar went to live in her father's house. (Gen. 38.11)

However, as the years passed and Shelah grew up, still Judah did not arrange for him to be married to Tamar. Tamar hatched an elaborate plan in which she disguised herself and had intercourse with Judah, who thought she was a prostitute. When Tamar's pregnancy was discovered, Judah's righteous anger was diffused when Tamar was able to prove that Judah was the father of her unborn children. Tamar also confronted Judah about how his inability to keep his promise had led her to such subterfuge. Tamar's resourcefulness in using the laws of lineage to her advantage earned her a place in the genealogy of Jesus through her twin sons, Zerah and Perez.

LEADERSHIP AS ORCHESTRATION

Rahab was a woman who knew her own worth. When she was presented with the opportunity to provide assistance to two men who had been sent to spy on her people's land, she discerned how she could be of help to them and at the same time save her own kith and kin in the invasion that she saw as inevitable.

> Then Joshua son of Nun sent two men secretly from Shittim as spies, saying, 'Go, view the land, especially Jericho.' So they went, and entered the house of a prostitute whose name was Rahab and spent the night there. (Josh. 2.1)

Rahab hid the spies from the king's men who had come looking for them. She helped them escape once she'd sent their pursuers in a different direction, and in return secured the promise that she and her family would not be harmed when the city fell into the hands of the Israelites. Rahab was politically astute and knew how to leverage her knowledge to protect her family.

Ruth's story is like Tamar's, one laced with the overtones of childless women and widows being left to the mercy of the rest of the community. Despite the complexity of cultural norms, Ruth and her mother-in-law survive a famine and work through their bitterness, disappointment and grief to find healing. Their careful attention enables them to leverage patriarchal customs to their advantage, and in Ruth's subsequent marriage and the bearing of children their status in the community is restored.

Bathsheba is referred to in Matthew's genealogy as 'the wife of Uriah', possibly a nod to how her husband as well as herself were wronged by King David when he chose to act on his lustful thoughts. David tried to cover his tracks after sleeping with Bathsheba by encouraging Uriah to leave the battlefield and be with his wife. However, Uriah's nobility far exceeded that of his king and he remained with his troops. King David then ensured that Uriah did not survive the fighting and subsequently took Bathsheba as his wife. Whatever Bathsheba's life was like as David's wife, she managed, as David lay impotent on his deathbed, to extract a promise that her son, Solomon, would be king. And throughout Solomon's reign, Bathsheba was by his side, queen mother extraordinaire, a woman with inordinate wisdom and insight.

The inclusion of these women in Jesus' genealogy provides some relief in the list of names and attests to their legacy as leaders, each in their own way, subverting cultural norms to make a difference for those whom they loved.

The Book of Chronicles is a particularly tedious read with all its lists of descendants and ancestors. There we also find that the focus is on the patriarchy with just a few exceptions. It is in these exceptions that we find, when we stop to look, incredible stories of women who are outstanding.

One of these exceptions is the mention of a woman named Sheerah. In 1 Chronicles, we learn that one of the descendants of Ephraim was a daughter, Sheerah, who built three cities!

> His daughter was Sheerah, who built both Lower and Upper Beth-horon, and Uzzen-sheerah. (1 Chron. 7.24)

In all of the many lists, this detail could so easily be missed as we gloss over yet another list of names. But the description of Sheerah as a builder of cities stops us in our tracks and demands our attention. Hers is a name whose story deserves further investigation. Sheerah built three cities, Lower Beth-horon, Upper Beth-horon and Uzzen-sheerah. Those are not accomplishments to be glossed over. No one just wakes up one morning and decides to build a city. That takes years of education, years of committed study, skilful manoeuvring in the echelons of craft guilds to secure a contract or three. And then careful planning, much consultation, the gathering of materials and workforce, and in all of this proving oneself to the sceptics who would surely abound when it became clear that the 'master builder' is a woman.

Looking into the back story of Sheerah's father reveals that his sons had been particularly corrupt and caused him much pain and sorrow. Later in life, he was blessed with a daughter, and it was she who brought him pride and joy. How remarkable must Sheerah have been to prevail in the way that she did in the midst of a culture predicated against her simply because of her gender?

And yet Sheerah was a builder of cities who used her skills to physically create something in which a community might thrive. Hers was the design and conception. Hers was the gathering together of a workforce. Hers was the gifting of a common purpose around which disparate folk might be brought together to cooperate, determining their future together. Hers was the vision, the drive, the expertise, as the giver of a focus in which many might find purpose. And hers was a legacy that served future generations. Sheerah saw the long game and chose to invest in it. Such investment requires confidence and security. Confidence in skills and ability and a security that does not depend on external validation. Often when women conceive a plan and invite others to be part of its execution, they risk the real possibility of others being credited with their hard work. They risk being overlooked when those who are more visible simply forget to attribute the foundations on which they build to their rightful instigator. And that is when an inner security enables peace with what has been accomplished.

Women can often find themselves working in the shadow of more visible men, their work used and sometimes abused to heighten another's profile. It is rare to find the efforts of male colleagues misappropriated in this way.

Many women have learned and may even have chosen to play second fiddle, quite simply putting community before self-promotion. There is, however, great power in playing second fiddle, demanding as it does a whole other set of gifts and skills that enhance communal effort.

Second Fiddle

The seconds occupy
a space inside
usually sandwiched between
more vocal parts
Their role to enhance
and amplify
all the beauty around
Contributing to the whole
in a nuanced, subtle way
Supporting
Bringing harmony
Interpreting another perspective
Providing a different insight
Navigating tricky rhythms and intervals
The seconds bring depth
and focus
Occasionally coming to the fore
but mostly remaining hidden
Often overlooked
and underestimated
More noticed by their absence
than their presence
Their gifts and skills
may be misunderstood
deemed less than
by those who lack perception
A cost they are willing to bear

MIRIAM'S SISTERS, DEBORAH'S DAUGHTERS

secure in their calling
not settling for less
but bringing more
And those who take the time
to affirm their gifts
and seek their accompaniment
are enriched by their giving
Caught up
and encircled
by a love that is fierce
in its passion
and clear in its mission
To contribute to the creation
of something whole
and worthwhile
a thing of beauty
birthed in playful improvisation
delivered in wondrous accord
The gift of second fiddle

7

Leadership as Survival

Men often ask me, 'Why are your female characters so paranoid?' It's not paranoia. It's recognition of their situation.
Margaret Atwood (1990)

It never fails to amaze me how often the biblical narratives pertaining to David, the shepherd boy who slayed the giant Goliath and then went on to become Israel's third king, are offered as stories of daring and adventure and lauded as tales of faith and devotion to God. The trail of devastation he left in his wake, mainly through exercising little sexual restraint or propriety, are legion.

Bathsheba and Tamar are just two of the women whose lives were irrevocably altered by encounters with David, and in their stories we are confronted by themes that continue to play out in many spheres of leadership today, not least in church leadership. David's story is a story of exceedingly bad behaviour being tolerated and even rewarded. It is a story of bad behaviour failing to be censured but, rather, perpetuated because it goes unchallenged at every stage. It is a story of those who are wronged being urged to keep quiet. It is a story of those who have the audacity to call out the bad behaviour being ostracized and shunned. It is a story of those who choose to turn the other way rather than confront wrongdoing. The stories of Bathsheba and Tamar are stories of rape and abuse that affect successive generations.

This part of David's reign of tyranny began when David saw a beautiful woman, Bathsheba, and wanted her. As king, David was accustomed to taking what he wanted and so he had intercourse with Bathsheba. When Bathsheba discovered that she was pregnant, she went to confront King David, her rapist. King David then set up an elaborate plot in an attempt to fool Bathsheba's husband, Uriah, into thinking the child was his. He encouraged Uriah to spend some time with his wife. However, Bathsheba's husband was too noble to abandon the troops with whom he was fighting. Foiled in that plot, David then engineered Uriah's death in battle so that Uriah would not uncover what David had done.

A little later, King David was confronted about his wrongdoing by the court prophet, Nathan. On being presented with the horror of his crimes, David appeared to show some contrition. But it was already too late. The damage was done. And David's son, Amnon, was about to follow in his father's footsteps.

Amnon had witnessed his father's example. So, when he decided that he simply must have his half-sister Tamar, he went right ahead and no one stopped him. The minute he got what he wanted, he cast her off. Tamar, however, refused to go quietly, and stuck around to haunt the corridors of the palace, loudly wailing, so that everyone was confronted by how she had been defiled. Of course, her wailing made people uncomfortable. Those onlookers did not want to bite the hand that fed them by sympathizing with Tamar's plight. So, even in the midst of her wretchedness, Tamar was admonished to be quiet. Her truth telling was silenced.

LEADERSHIP AS SURVIVAL

At every juncture of these stories there were other options. At every turn there was the possibility for redemption or for a different ending. Too many people refused to intervene. Too many were willing simply to turn a blind eye. And that allowed wrongdoing to be perpetuated from generation to generation.

Tamar did what she could in the moment to confront the abuse by refusing to disappear quietly.

Bathsheba's was more of a long game. The son that was conceived out of rape died. But, as we saw earlier, as the now impotent king lay on his deathbed, Bathsheba, with the help of Nathan the prophet, managed to extract a promise that one of Bathsheba and David's other sons, Solomon, would be king rather than the son who raped Tamar. And when Solomon took up his throne, he set his mother, Bathsheba, at his right hand. This became a precedent for queen mothers in the generations that followed in that monarchy. Bathsheba also took her place in the ancestry of Jesus.

These stories of Bathsheba and Tamar unveil for us the culture in which they were written as violent and abusive. Although heavily redacted, they still manage to convey for us stories of leadership turned feral. And I wonder whether they also hold up for us a mirror in which we see reflected so vividly stories of abuse of people and of power that continue to be perpetrated today, particularly when people turn the other way and persist in trying to redeem abusers by telling of the good things they also achieved. How often do we hear of the great gifts and achievements of David, warrior, king and poet? When we attempt to mitigate the actions of those who are flawed by lauding their achievements, we deepen the wounds borne by victims and survivors.

A vital task of leadership today is that of breaking patterns that are set to be repeated. Moving beyond survival to bringing abusers to justice. That work consists in listening to the survivors, in encouraging and protecting whistleblowers and not just listening to those who have power, a platform and a voice. Every time another abusive leadership scandal is made public, it is striking how many people have known and simply kept quiet or, perhaps worse, made easy excuses for bad behaviour. And, even in the face of incontrovertible evidence, when stories begin to emerge, still many of those affected are silenced so that 'influencers' may be heard, which means that fewer victims' stories shape the narrative while other victims experience another form of silencing along with the clear signal that some stories matter more than others.

Bathsheba and Tamar's stories are stories of survival and of the refusal to be defined by the abuse to which they were subjected. However, the men who perpetrated such violence were enabled to go on and continue to abuse women, and in King David's case to have his story hailed as one of heroic leadership, with many of the less palatable aspects reframed for posterity.

May we learn to honour survivors without in any way glorifying the trauma they have endured. And may we seek to bring perpetrators of abuse to justice.

There is also work to be done in teaching our young people the importance of appropriate boundaries and in giving them the confidence to enforce them.

I vividly remember an event at a Sunday night worship service I occasionally attended. The church was filled with young people, the preaching was fiery, there were lots of people 'caught up in the spirit'. Then I found myself surrounded. My arms were being held and I was being prayed for. At one point, the elderly pastor of the church joined our group, and as he prayed

LEADERSHIP AS SURVIVAL

he was thumping on my chest, exhorting me to 'Let go, lassie, let go. Let the Spirit in.' Although I was sore for a few days after that, it did not occur to me then that his actions were inappropriate. Such was the culture fostered in that environment, that boundaries became extremely porous and any questioning of what happened in worship would have been met with outrage. My faith would have been questioned and I would have been ostracized. As I recall that incident, I am struck by how bizarre it sounds. But I am also struck by how little awareness I had of being violated and of how powerless I was to advocate for myself, far less for others.

Perhaps unsurprisingly, David's tyranny of horror continued apace. Having succeeded Saul to the throne, David inherited and continued the feuds and bloodletting that were prevalent in a culture of fragility and territorial strife. During a time of famine while he reigned, David enquired of God why the land was so afflicted and learned that it was because Saul had failed to honour a treaty with the Gibeonites. David decided that this must be rectified and asked the Gibeonites how that might be done. The Gibeonites asked for the lives of seven men from Saul's lineage as atonement. David, keen to appease the vengeful rendition of the God whom he revered, acquiesced to their demand. The seven men were killed and impaled for all to see. Rizpah, who had been one of Saul's concubines, was the mother of two of those men killed. She began a vigil by the bodies so that they would not be devoured by birds or wild animals. Her actions shamed King David into, eventually, arranging burial for the bodies. As soon as the bodies were buried, the famine ended. Rizpah, however, continued to carry in her body the wounds inflicted by men who knew only violence as a way to a fragile peace.

We may want to consign such violence to a historical or mythological context that prevailed when humanity knew no better, where borders were frequently contested and where peace was always fragile. And yet, all over the world today, women still keep vigil over the bodies of their sons, killed by violence in territorial disputes while peace still drowns in blood-run streets. And weary and despairing people avert their eyes to maintain their sanity.

Leadership consists in developing skills of survival, but it also involves rooting out the evil that maligns peace and values human life only as collateral in wars waged locally and globally. May we keep vigil with all who weep today.

Rizpah

Rizpah
kept vigil
bearing witness
as the bodies of her sons rotted
Bearing witness
as the buzzards circled
Bearing witness
as the stench attracted animals
who wanted to devour the corpses
already devoured by death
Another mother compelled to keep vigil
by the broken body of her child
Another mother joining countless mothers
throughout the world
whose children are killed by violence
Violence sanctioned by state
or discounted by white supremacy
or mitigated by claiming 'extenuating' circumstance
A mother's child
deemed expendable
for a greater good
Rizpah's vigil shamed the king
into arranging burial
Her desolation and devotion
could never be extinguished
She carried for evermore in her body
the violence done to her child
a trauma borne by women
whose bodies remember

8

Leadership as Turning Things Around

'Won't You be My Sister?'
Hear me as a woman.
Amanda Gorman (2022)

It has been suggested that the Book of Judges in the Hebrew Scriptures was essentially an account of all the depravity and lawlessness that existed when the children of Israel did not have a monarchy in place. Perhaps that's why we rarely hear it read in churches.

Throughout this part of Scripture, we hear repeated requests for a king to be established to rule over the people. As it happened, many of their kings did not provide good moral leadership either, but Judges does contain many awful stories from before the monarchic era.

One of these horrific stories is recounted in Judges 11.29–40, the story of Jephthah and his unnamed daughter. Jephthah is a man with a sorry past. He was evicted from his father's home by his half-brothers because he was born of another woman to whom his father was not married. He lived rough and gathered around him a bunch of marauding raiders. How much Jephthah's experience of rejection and bullying affected his later actions is a matter about which we may well speculate, but his marauding life contained little sign of redemption. Known for his prowess in skirmishes, he was invited to lead the troops in Gilead. He found himself facing a battle with the Ammonites. For some seemingly inexplicable reason, before engaging in battle, Jephthah made a vow to God that if God helped him to victory he would sacrifice, as a thanksgiving offering, whoever came to meet him from the doors of his house when he returned from battle. A professional mercenary, Jephthah was indeed victorious in battle and made his way home remembering his vow. It so happened that it was his daughter and only child who came to meet him with music and dancing to celebrate that her beloved father was safely home. A salutary greeting for a man with a vow to honour. As you might expect, the father blamed his daughter for having the audacity to greet his return, telling her that she has brought him low and become a great trouble for him. We see this familiar trope of victim blaming played out time and again in violence against women. When a woman is violated, it's because she was in the wrong place at the wrong time, or incorrectly dressed, or adopted the wrong attitude, or any number of reasons that make violence inevitable.

Jephthah's daughter, with far more grace and strength than her father, acknowledged his vow and accepted her fate, with one request. She asked that she be allowed a couple of months to wander the mountains with her friends, bewailing her virginity. And so she and her friends took off to acknowledge all the experiences that she now could not have and to bewail her impending death. And in two months she returned to meet her fate.

I've always been intrigued by that young woman's actions of choosing to live before she died. There is also something powerful in the story of her friends who were willing to accompany her as she wandered those hills, bearing witness to her grief, accompanying her in her mourning, and who established a tradition of remembering her sacrifice with other young women for four days every year thereafter.

For many years I served in health care chaplaincy, often accompanying others as they faced their own mortality. Those folk I accompanied taught me how to live.

Folk like Ellen, who having lost her mobility and the power of speech dictated a book for her loved ones, blinking her eyes as they took her through the alphabet, letter by letter – like Jean-Dominique Bauby in *The Diving Bell and the Butterfly* (1997). Her determination and their love ensured that Ellen's stories were not lost to future generations of her family.

Or like Eileen, a devout Anglican with whom I'd built up a relationship as she weathered a prolonged stay in hospital. Eileen burst my bubble of pomposity by asking me to shave her chin on the night she died rather than requesting that I offer any more recognizable sacrament that I may have anticipated. Eileen surely taught me that there are many ways to smooth the journey back to God. The sacredness of a small act offered with great love, to paraphrase Mother Teresa, made the holy ground on which we stood shimmer with the presence of angels that night.

And Maureen, a woman I'd only known for four days, who each time I visited described to me beautiful portraits of those she would encounter in the afterlife that she was convinced awaited her. I happened to be with her as she passed from one life to another, a moment in which I envisaged Maureen shrugging off her cosy cardigan to put on a floaty dress and some heels before striding purposefully into the company that awaited her and whose company she anticipated with joy.

None of these lessons were presented with bullet points or pie charts or graphs, or even with catchy slogans or acronyms. But all hit home and left a lasting impression that precipitated change in me, and I like to think continue to make a difference for me and for those I serve.

The story of Jephthah's daughter also demonstrates something of how far a daughter was prepared to go to honour the vow her father had made in extreme foolishness.

There is another story of a woman saving male pride in 1 Samuel 22, the story of Abigail. Abigail is married to a lout of a man by the name of Nabal. Nabal is a materially rich man, with many sheep and goats, but with the characteristics of a common thug. As he and his men worked among their flocks, they were approached by David's men to share a part of their bounty for an upcoming feast day, a seemingly reasonable request in a culture that prided itself on its hospitality. Nabal not only refused to share but he threw shadow on David's reputation as a local hero. Nabal's dismissal brought imminent danger to his whole household as David prepared to salvage his pride and to retaliate by commanding his men to get ready to destroy the household that had so disrespected him. One of Nabal's shepherds managed to alert Abigail to what had transpired, knowing that if anyone could avert disaster it was Abigail. The shepherd's hopes were fulfilled as Abigail made plans to intercede. Abigail swiftly gathered a bounty of produce and sent it ahead of her to placate David, before meeting him herself. When she met David, she didn't waste time apologizing for her feckless husband, but instead asked forgiveness for her own behaviour in not being aware of the emissaries David had sent. It's always disarming when someone leads with an apology. But Abigail went even further. She also managed to paint herself as an escape route for David by suggesting that she had been provided as divine intervention to prevent David from having blood on his hands, a stain that would have lingered if he had acted on impulse and killed Nabal and Abigail's household in anger. Something that would not bode well for a king in waiting. Abigail enacted a piece of calculated, skilful rhetoric that served its purpose. David was flattered and sufficiently distracted from his wrath, and Abigail earned herself a place in the future king's respect, a respect that would soon be honoured when Nabal died and David took Abigail as his wife.

Sometimes leadership looks a lot like stepping up to avert crisis. Not wasting time apportioning blame or decrying others but simply taking the reins to ensure that things move forward. Learning the lessons of the past may prove useful but taking stock to ascertain what is possible now enables the future to be secured.

Shrouds

Shrouds are for the dead
For covering up decaying remains
They do not transform
They only mask
And underneath erosion continues
until in time only an outline endures
a hint of something once treasured and loved
remaining only in memories and myths
that have become another form of shroud
through which it is impossible
to distinguish truth

In a season when our rituals of faith
are shrouded in mystery
weighed down by tradition
dare we peel back those shrouds?
Dare we lift a corner
to peek beneath
and recognize
before it is too late
those things that may have served us well
in a dim and distant past
but that should be left now
to their natural demise?
Dare we name aloud
a new truth for a new season?
A light for today's darkness?

MIRIAM'S SISTERS, DEBORAH'S DAUGHTERS

Dare we step away
from tiptoeing around the dead weights
and chart a new direction
that heads towards light and life?
Brush off the stray threads that still cling
whose filaments, though slender, hold us back?
Dare we take good long freeing strides
that carry us on to a new threshold
where we are greeted by joy
and carried in love?
And, resolving not to look back
or yearn for the comfort of the familiar
by which we were weighed down
discover the new territory
that awaits with the promise
of a new course
for a new world
where these three remain
Faith, hope and love

9

Leadership as Resistance

My movement is my movement. When all the dust has settled on the groundbreaking-ness, I'm still going to be doing this.
Lizzo (2022)

I was once accused of 'bringing the church into disrepute' by using my social media platform to counter some of the patriarchal, misogynistic 'banter' that I experienced in church courts. I knew that a full-frontal attack would be futile and only cause me further grief, so I told the truth with humour on social media. At no point did I identify or shame the perpetrators. Writing was simply my way of processing the hurt. Sadly, that gave rise to an attempt by some powerful men, who felt threatened by my writing, to take action to confront me about what they perceived as misdemeanours, threatening that they had cause to begin a disciplinary procedure. They quickly realized that, in fact, to do so would only expose the underlying culture of bullying and misogyny that prevailed, so a new 'policy' was concocted and placed on the statutes aimed at curtailing clergy's use of social media. What became clear is that these men would prefer to make decrees and police social media platforms rather than confront their own bad behaviour and insecurity.

It is said that 'hard cases make bad laws'. I wonder how

often those bad laws have been legislated by powerful men who were threatened by a woman calling out their inappropriate behaviour.

Queen Vashti was one such woman. Her king, who was quite literally 'entertaining the troops', ordered her to appear for their delectation as a way of exhibiting his great wealth and fortune. Queen Vashti refused to be paraded before the enclave of the great and the good, gathered by her husband and with whom he had been partying for more than six months. She refused to condone his antics. She refused to become an exhibit of her husband's warped view of power and success. She also refused to risk her own safety by entering an arena full of well-inebriated men to whom the king had given license to behave as they pleased.

Queen Vashti said, 'No!'

Well, the rumour mill roared into action. The news of Queen Vashti's defiance was told around every women's gathering place, down by the river as laundry was done, or around the well as the animals were watered. The story of the queen who said 'No' was shared from province to province. And fragile male egos were so threatened that a new law was passed – that all women must do whatever their husbands said.

There is a curious pattern that often unfolds in response to rules that curtail freedom. Initially, folk will be generally compliant. Through time, however, resistance kicks in, the authority of those who make demands is questioned, and the insecurity that has instigated curtailment is seen for what it is – an attempt to maintain or retain power and control. And in all those places where folk have been silenced, truth telling when it erupts does so often in destructive ways.

We are witnessing some of that currently in the UK as enquiries into the government's response to the Covid pandemic uncover the duplicity, lies and corrupt acts of many who held power. When people begin to see what lies at the heart of some of the controlling pronouncements made, there is a ripple effect that is beyond the control of those whose hold on power is maintained through subterfuge. There is solidarity and a sense of common purpose in joining forces with others who have been wronged. The recent and ongoing Post Office scandal in the UK – where those who managed Post Offices were wrongly accused of fraud when a bug-ridden computer system was at fault – has exposed a huge amount of cover-up and corruption in the echelons of power. It took a lot of persistence and protesting of innocence before a review was instigated and the truth was brought to light. And even in the face of clear evidence of wrongful prosecution and conviction, it took the making and broadcast of a television drama to share the story and garner momentum for an overturning of convictions.

For change to be effected in any arena someone has to lead the way and, by so doing, encourage others to follow suit. Change requires a movement that disrupts the status quo, that gathers momentum and that offers different opportunities for others to get on board. Early adopters are needed as well as those who wait a while and join the movement a bit later when they are more convinced of its efficacy and appreciate the importance of maintaining the momentum.

In the example of Queen Vashti, her defiance could have remained an isolated incident. However, in the events that followed – in the search for a new queen, in countering the insecurity of men in power, in alerting the king to the evil in his midst, in halting the oppression of the newly installed Queen Esther's people – all were inspired by that single act of defiance that set in motion a whole revolution. Others took up the cause and not only were laws instituted but practices were changed.

An oft-quoted verse from Esther would seem to support that notion of a cascade of events, each informing and enabling another:

> 'For if you keep silent at this time, relief and deliverance will rise for the Jews from another quarter, but you and your father's family will perish. Who knows? Perhaps you have come to royal dignity for just such a time as this.' (Est. 4.14)

Leaders are called not just to make sense of unfolding events in hindsight, but to read the room so that appropriate and timely intervention may be offered as momentum builds and a tipping point is reached that precipitates change.

Although Queen Vashti receives scant mention in Hebrew Scripture, her courage set the stage for Queen Esther to be in the right place at the right time. And Vashti's defiance surely gave the king cause to wonder how his relationship with his queen might be vastly different, a difference he began to fashion with Esther whose shrewdness far outstripped that of her king.

Many movements that have changed the world have begun with a single act, seemingly insignificant on its own, that became a catalyst for momentous change.

One of the pieces of work I led in the Church of Scotland was Path of Renewal – accompanying leaders and congregations through transition. The tagline of Path of Renewal was: 'A movement, not a programme.' Movements seek to recover core purpose, to discover what are the immutable values of a community and to work out how to live into those values to make a difference.

LEADERSHIP AS RESISTANCE

Many institutions have grown out of good and noble and sometimes radical intentions to provide services – religion, finance, education, health. The National Health Service in the UK sought to provide health care for all, free at the point of delivery.

The challenge is that, once institutions become established, the radical nature of their instigation and their core values become obscured, not least by bureaucracy and by other competing interests. In response to this, movements arise on the margins that seek to challenge the stagnation or status quo of institutions in an attempt to recover those radical principles on which they were founded. However, in an institution there arises a lot of extraneous paraphernalia, things that may be useful for maintaining an institution but are not fit for purpose in delivering or engaging with the core purpose of the organization, and there will often be a struggle to maintain the status quo that protects those elements of an institution, particularly when status or employment is at stake.

In the main, movements have to be constantly pitted against institutions. Occasionally, the institution sees the value of a movement and offers collaboration to help the institution restore core purposes, but more often than not movements are opposed. Those who participate in movements find their values critically examined by others. While this might appear threatening, it can prove helpful in honing and defining the purpose of a movement. It also helps those engaged in the movement to consciously embody the changes they want to effect.

In the stories of the Exodus of God's people from Egypt, we see God's people being transformed by the re-establishment of God's will and purpose in their lives individually and in community. As they became settled in a new land, institutions grew up, a longed-for monarchy was established and corruption set in. Prophets then emerged to challenge those institutions and to lead new movements that re-established the core purposes of the people of God – to live in God's peaceable kingdom seeking the prosperity of the land in which they dwelled by loving justice, practising mercy and walking humbly with God.

Similarly, we see Jesus and his disciples engaged in a kingdom movement, challenging the political and religious authorities of the day. And what a movement – one that embraced prostitutes and tax collectors, that encouraged parties but that also promoted focusing on the inner life – feeding body, mind and spirit!

The vitality of the Church demands that such movements, birthed by the Holy Spirit, remain active in communities today – embodied, contagious, always willing to challenge institutions by focusing on renewal, inspiring others to re-define core values and how those might be lived out in our different cultures.

Movements, though they must remain mobile and light on their feet, responsive to new insight and revelation, also require resilience and a commitment to the long term. Change, particularly cultural change, is an ambitious endeavour and slow to effect. Those who participate must find ways of being both internally and externally resourced. Queen Esther adapted her spiritual practices for her context and gradually engineered that she would be in the right place at the right time to make a difference. Reading the room served her well, along with the courage and compassion she embodied as she effected change. But I wonder what might have happened if Queen Vashti had not said 'No'?

'No' is a Complete Sentence

Vashti shares her wise counsel with Esther

Exile
is preferable
to any compromise
that might have been expected of me
My life would have been worthless
if I'd surrendered to the drunken masses
who kept company with the king
My banishment made way
for your victory
I like to think
that when the penny dropped
and the king came to understand
that 'No' is a complete sentence
he felt just a little remorse
and resolved in future
to be more attentive to his consorts
I like to think
that paved the way for you
to make your petitions
and to harness his power
to save your people
Nothing motivated by love
is ever wasted
I have no regrets

MIRIAM'S SISTERS, DEBORAH'S DAUGHTERS

Rather, I count myself blessed
without fear or compromise
to champion a woman's right
to say 'No'

10

Leadership as Prophetic

As we observed earlier, Bathsheba established a precedence of queen mothers taking up important roles alongside their sons as they reigned in Judah. So it was that Jedidah – mother of Josiah, who took the throne at the tender age of eight years old – guided her son and proved a positive influence in his life. Josiah's father was considered an apostate and did not serve in any way as a positive role model. It was his death that precipitated Josiah's accession to the throne. His mother stepped in to guide her son as he embraced his roles and responsibilities as king. It is recorded that Josiah was faithful to the law of Moses and the ways established by him, and faithful to the God of the Israelites, qualities that could only have been fostered by his mother. Josiah, during his reign, was engaged in sweeping reforms that saw the dismantling of altars to other gods and the return to worshipping one God as well as being involved in restoring the temple.

When his officials approached him with a scroll found in the early stages of the temple restoration, Josiah, on hearing the message of the scroll, was convinced – to such an extent that he rent his clothes. He recognized that, as the scroll decreed, there would be a price to pay for the years the Israelites had spent neglecting God. He sought the advice of Huldah the prophet, not to have the scroll authenticated, but to seek her counsel on what he and his people should do next in a bid to appease the God who, according to the scroll, was intent on their destruction. Huldah spoke truth without fear. She advised the king that, though judgement would not be avoided, and the people would be destroyed because of their ancestors' sins, he himself would not see that destruction but would die in peace. As it happened, this prophecy was not fulfilled because of Josiah's later defiance in disguising himself to engage in a battle that he was advised not to enter. However, Josiah did continue reforms that ensured that the people would once again follow the one God of their ancestors.

Huldah's appearance in the text is brief but it is recorded twice for posterity, in 2 Kings 22.8–20 and 2 Chronicles 44.1–28. We know little of what Huldah did before or after this account. Nonetheless hers was a very powerful intervention. What does seem clear is that she had somehow earned her stripes in being the prophet from whom Josiah would seek wise counsel. There is no suggestion that Huldah was approached because other prophets were unavailable, but rather that she was Josiah's preferred option (2 Kings 22.14). Both Jeremiah and Zephaniah were her contemporaries, but it was to Huldah that Josiah sent his very distinguished delegation.

Huldah did not shirk her prophetic calling. It takes courage to speak truth to power and Huldah may have been tempted to disguise the truth, to sweeten it somehow. Instead, she proved faithful to her calling as a prophet of God, mediating the message of God.

Although Josiah already knew, when the words of the scroll were read to him, that this was the word of the Lord, Huldah's

LEADERSHIP AS PROPHETIC

testimony to the words and her verification played a vital role in authenticating what would become an important canonical scripture.

Huldah is one of only a handful of women in Hebrew Scripture who is described as a prophet, the others being Miriam, Deborah, an unnamed woman in Isaiah (nameless although significant enough to have a child with Isaiah) and Noadiah, a woman believed to have led the charge in opposing the wall building of Nehemiah (Gafney, 2008).

The prophetic role of speaking truth to power is a vital role today and the women who are willing to take up that mantle are legion. Like the prophets of old, it is a gruelling role to be held for a season until the baton can be passed on. Women have led the way in demonstrating how to step into prophetic leadership and then step back. In recent years, we have seen many high-profile women, like New Zealand's PM Jacinda Ardern, Scotland's First Minister Nicola Sturgeon and YouTube's CEO Susan Wojcicki, who have demonstrated exemplary leadership and commitment and know when it's time to say 'Enough'. Survival in the kind of hostile, combative environments that surround their role rests on knowing when to pass on the reins to others. This is not failure; it is good role modelling for all who follow, signalling that demanding roles that involve giving our all cannot be sustained indefinitely. Until the arena changes, there is work to be done on developing those who will follow and who will know when it is time to step back and let others take the strain. Prophetic leadership is leadership for a season.

Unholy Trinity

Prophets
Willing to speak truth to power
Willing to call out injustice
Willing to draw attention to the plight of those on the margins
whose voices are not heard and whose cries go unheeded
Accomplices of Poets
who describe a better way
Who put into words a vision of inclusion
A vision in which nothing is right side up
and where influence is found in the least and the last
Alongside Dreamers
who remind us that transformation is possible
who reimagine a future that is not yet but will be
An unholy Trinity those three
Prophets, Poets, Dreamers
who mark out the thresholds and stand in gateways
and remind us there are no margins
in the inclusive kingdom
of Prophets, Poets and Dreamers
So may it be

11

Leadership as Song

We have only one rule and that is there are no rules, so stand up and sing as much as you want to.
Natalie Maines (2022)

When Mary travelled to spend time with her cousin, Elizabeth, who was also pregnant, we get a glimpse into Mary's wisdom and her incredible insight into the part she was called to play in her people's liberation. Living in occupied territory, under an oppressive regime, and pregnant out of wedlock in an unforgiving culture, Mary was yet readily able to identify with the themes of hope and promise that were woven into her people's faith.

When she arrived at Elizabeth's house, the child in the womb of her cousin leapt in recognition of the child that Mary carried, a fleeting glimpse of all that was to come as Elizabeth's child, John, heralded the advent of Jesus, the Messiah.

And Mary was moved to song.

In her song are traces not just of all that she has absorbed from her faith and her culture – a longing for freedom from all that her people have endured alongside the promise of deliverance – but a portent of the future. The portent of freedom was wrought at a price, as those in power wreak the worst kinds of havoc to retain their supremacy when under threat. Mary's song encapsulates the incredible, faithful resilience of her people, who in the depths of their suffering recall the faithfulness of God in the past and the potential of God's favour in the present, and wholly trust in God's redemption for the future. This is her song:

> And Mary said,
> 'My soul magnifies the Lord,
> and my spirit rejoices in God my Saviour,
> for he has looked with favour on the lowly state of his servant.
> Surely from now on all generations will call me blessed,
> for the Mighty One has done great things for me,
> and holy is his name;
> indeed, his mercy is for those who fear him
> from generation to generation.
> He has shown strength with his arm;
> he has scattered the proud in the imagination of their hearts.
> He has brought down the powerful from their thrones
> and lifted up the lowly;
> he has filled the hungry with good things
> and sent the rich away empty.
> He has come to the aid of his child Israel,
> in remembrance of his mercy,
> according to the promise he made to our ancestors,
> to Abraham and to his descendants forever.'
> (Luke 1.46–55)

Mary's song echoes that of Hannah, her forebear who haunted the temple day and night, praying for a child. So distraught was Hannah when she prayed that she was accused of being drunk. The pain of Hannah's childlessness was exacerbated by the fertility of her husband's other wife, Penninah, who had borne him children. Although it appears that Hannah knew herself loved in her relationship, her childlessness remained a source of great pain for her and her husband. The narrative rendered by patriarchal voices would have us believe that Hannah and Penninah were enemies. Perhaps they were. Perhaps, as was the custom, Penninah was brought into play after ten years of Hannah's childless marriage, and taunted Hannah about her barrenness. It is also possible that Penninah was brought in precisely at the suggestion of Hannah to provide the children that she couldn't and to enable her to remain in the loving relationship she knew. Perhaps both women were caught up in a culture that pitted one against the other, and together they found a way to subvert that expectation as they supported one another through love, life and loss.

Hannah continued to pray for a child and when her hopes were realized and she delivered her firstborn son, she sang a song of praise to God. The themes of her song – rejoicing in God and hoping in the salvation of God that would see fortunes overturned and justice re-distributed – find their echo in Mary's song. Both women sang out their faith and bore it in their womb. Both women bore sons who played significant roles in the story of the people of God. Hannah went on to have another five children, two daughters and three more sons. This first son, as she had promised, she dedicated to God. He was Samuel who became the last judge in Israel before the monarchy, for which the people pleaded with God, was established.

Hannah's song is recorded in 1 Samuel:

Hannah prayed and said,
'My heart exults in the Lord;

MIRIAM'S SISTERS, DEBORAH'S DAUGHTERS

my strength is exalted in my God.
My mouth derides my enemies
because I rejoice in your victory.
There is no Holy One like the Lord,
no one besides you;
there is no Rock like our God.
Talk no more so very proudly;
let not arrogance come from your mouth,
for the Lord is a God of knowledge,
and by him actions are weighed.
The bows of the mighty are broken,
but the feeble gird on strength.
Those who were full have hired themselves out for bread,
but those who were hungry are fat with spoil.
The barren has borne seven,
but she who has many children is forlorn.
The Lord kills and brings to life;
he brings down to Sheol and raises up.
The Lord makes poor and makes rich;
he brings low; he also exalts.
He raises up the poor from the dust;
he lifts the needy from the ash heap
to make them sit with princes
and inherit a seat of honour.
For the pillars of the earth are the Lord's,
and on them he has set the world.
He will guard the feet of his faithful ones,
but the wicked will perish in darkness,
for not by might does one prevail.
The Lord! His adversaries will be shattered;
the Most High will thunder in heaven.

LEADERSHIP AS SONG

The Lord will judge the ends of the earth;
he will give strength to his king
and exalt the power of his anointed.'
(1 Sam. 2.1–10)

A third song in Scripture is attributed to Deborah and her partner in arms, Barak. The only female judge recorded in Hebrew Scripture, Deborah is also attributed with being a prophet. As God's intermediary, Deborah discerns the right time to go to war with the Canaanites and summons the leader of her armies, Barak. He will only agree to go to battle if Deborah goes with him. Deborah readily does so but warns Barak that a woman will be credited with destroying Sisera, the commander of the Canaanite army. Perhaps Barak assumed that woman would be Deborah. However, the story goes on to tell how Sisera managed to escape, abandoning his troops. As he made his way back to his mother who was waiting for him to return with his spoils of war, Sisera took refuge in the tent of Jael who, as we saw in Chapter 4, despatched him with a tent peg as he slept off his exertion. A cautionary tale for those who exhort women to be 'more biblical' in nature.

Together, Deborah and Barak sing a song of victory:

'In the days of Shamgar son of Anath,
in the days of Jael, caravans ceased
and travellers kept to the byways.
The peasantry prospered in Israel,
they grew fat on plunder,
because you arose, Deborah,
arose as a mother in Israel.
When new gods were chosen,

then war was in the gates.
Was shield or spear to be seen
among forty thousand in Israel?
My heart goes out to the commanders of Israel
who offered themselves willingly among the people.
Bless the Lord.
Tell of it, you who ride on white donkeys,
you who sit on rich carpets,
and you who walk by the way.
To the sound of musicians at the watering places,
there they repeat the triumphs of the Lord,
the triumphs of his peasantry in Israel.
Then down to the gates marched the people of the Lord.
Awake, awake, Deborah!
Awake, awake, utter a song!
Arise, Barak, lead away your captives,
O son of Abinoam.'
(Judges 5.6–12)

The song is a lengthy one and may comprise the oldest part of Hebrew Scripture. A fitting tribute to Deborah, whose tenure as judge brought peace for a generation.

The fourth song recorded in Scripture is the song in which Miriam led the women after they crossed the Red Sea on their flight from Egypt. Like the song of Deborah and Barak, it is a triumphant hymn of victory:

Then the prophet Miriam, Aaron's sister, took a tambourine in her hand; and all the women went out after her with tambourines and with dancing. And Miriam sang to them:

> 'Sing to the Lord, for he has triumphed gloriously;
> horse and rider he has thrown into the sea.'
> (Ex. 15.20–21)

In my imagination, these words are a refrain, sung in response to a narrated version of the escape from Egypt such as that recounted in the preceding verses, Exodus 15.1–18, attributed to Moses.

When women's voices are refused a hearing in other ways, there is something of the power of a song that has the potential to become an earworm that nonetheless lives on and tells a story worth remembering.

Each of these songs embraces the opportunity to celebrate the covenant relationship that God has with humanity and to frame events through that interpretive lens. They echo the subversive nature of the justice of God and act as placeholders in times when that justice seems distant. Embracing the hymnody of these biblical women prepares us to seek justice today.

But no consideration of song in Scripture would be complete without considering the Song of Songs, which is the Song of Solomon 1.1.

The only parts of the song I can recall hearing from youth church days are:

> He brought me to the banqueting house,
> and his intention toward me was love.
> (S. of Sol. 2.4)

These words became an oft-requested chorus that we sang in youth church. Clearly, those who shepherded me in faith toned down the possibilities in the Song of Songs, choosing to read it, as many have done, as an allegory of Christ's love for the world.

In later years, folk would ask to have some verses from the Song of Solomon read as part of their marriage service:

> Set me as a seal upon your heart,
> as a seal upon your arm;
> for love is strong as death,
> passion as fierce as the grave.
> Its flashes are flashes of fire,
> a raging flame.
> Many waters cannot quench love,
> neither can floods drown it.
> (S. of Sol. 8.6–7)

The Song of Solomon is worthy of much more scrutiny than it is often afforded.

In the song we encounter a woman or girl described as Shulamite. This girl is uncensored when she speaks of her love, fulsome in her desire and unafraid to ask for what she wants in sexual fulfilment. The song has been used in a variety of ways throughout its existence – as a wedding song, as a celebration of blackness, it appears in literature and in film. It would seem that no matter how much the Church seeks to tone down the Song of Solomon and sanitize the Shulamite girl, her exuberance and zest for life and love will not be hidden under the bedclothes of propriety but will continue to escape and tantalize the righteous with an unquenchable passion. Any woman who can articulate her raw sexuality as well as the Shulamite girl deserves a hearing.

Leadership is accompanied by song, be it protest song, war song or love song.

God Bearers

In the womb of a woman
are the seeds of all the songs she will need
for her sojourn through life
A song of love
that rings clear and true
voicing all that she offers
and all that she desires
to keep love alive
A song of hope
that is borne in the dreams that she harbours
for generations yet unborn
to know the beauty of peace
A song of faith
that resonates clear and long
from the foundations of the world
A song of protest
that yearns for justice
for the lowly to be lifted up
and the oppressed to be free
Seeds of all the songs
that will bring to birth
abundant life today

12

Leadership as Tenacity

The most common way people give up their power is by thinking they don't have any.
Alice Walker (in conversation)

As Mary's willingness to submit to the will of God is emphasized by those who tell her story, her strength of character often becomes diminished in the telling, her temerity is overshadowed by her purity, and her intuitive resilience is left in the dust of history.

There are many Christmas card depictions of Mary that portray her as a fairly insipid character, surrounded by angels and shepherds that might have emerged from a children's Nativity play.

But some of my favourite depictions of Mary are those in which she is defeating the powers of evil.

She is sometimes portrayed as crushing the head of the serpent with her heel in response to the verse in the Book of Genesis:

> I will put enmity between you and the woman and between your offspring and hers; he will strike your head, and you will strike his heel. (Gen. 3.15)

Another portrayal, from a thirteenth-century manuscript, the 'De Brailes Hours', has an image of Mary punching the devil in the face in order to retrieve a charter by which a priest named Theophilus had sold his soul to the devil.

My favourite is from the fourteenth-century illuminated manuscript the 'Taymouth Hours', named after the castle where it was kept, in which the Angel Gabriel is holding the infant Jesus while Mary wrestles Satan to the ground. I imagine Mary enlisting Gabriel's help by saying 'Here, hold the baby' before getting stuck in!

All of this is by way of recovering the strength of character of Mary, mother of Jesus, mother of God, a strength borne out in her intuitive wisdom and in her resilience in confronting pain and sorrow.

Mary's intuition is captured initially in her response to the angel who visited to tell her she would bear in her womb God's son. Having listened carefully to the angel's pitch, she discerns the hand of God and agrees to the part she will play. Patriarchal narratives will describe Mary's assent as the submissive act of someone too young to do otherwise. In the light of how we observe Mary later, taking a decisive role in the life of her son, remaining with him until the bitter end, it is unlikely that she was as naive as history often portrays her.

Her intuition in the early stages of her pregnancy led her to visit Elizabeth, her older relative who was also carrying a child. Elizabeth's child would play a vital role in the purposes of God, preparing a way in the wilderness for the one who was to come – namely Jesus the Messiah whom Mary was carrying. It was while she was with Elizabeth that Mary spoke most powerfully of her understanding of the immensity of the honour (and responsibility) bestowed on her in the words of the Magnificat (Luke

1.46–55), as we have seen. In those prophetic words she demonstrated her insight into how the child she carried would bring about the defeat of evil and of the pride of Empire while raising up those whose lives were a constant struggle for survival.

We see that intuition exercised again when Jesus was presented in the temple (Luke 2.22–40) and Mary heard, in the words of Simeon and Anna, confirmation of the role of Jesus as Messiah and of how that would be resisted by the powerful who had much to lose in any new order. It is in these encounters that we grasp something of Mary's insight into the pain that she will endure as a mother who will be forced to witness the torture and execution of her son.

Early in John's Gospel, there is another encounter with Mary's intuitive nature – at the wedding at Cana in Galilee (John 2.1–11), Mary, on hearing that the wine has run out, alerts Jesus to the plight of the wedding hosts. Jesus resists the possibility that he might be involved in alleviating this calamity. Mary, however, despite Jesus' resistance, instructs the servants to do whatever he might tell them. Although Jesus is not aware that it is time for him to step up, Mary his mother is. She trusts her instincts and prepares the ground.

Intuition is an undervalued quality in leadership. As demonstrated in Mary, intuition when harnessed alongside courage and tenacity has powerful impact.

Alongside her powerful intuition Mary displays tenacity as she mothers God's son, seeing him both fêted and maligned, revered and abhorred, cherished and despised. And like too many mothers throughout the world, she is forced to endure her son's brutal murder. To all of this, she gave her informed consent.

Mary, Mother of God

When Mary pushed her son
from her womb
into the waiting arms of the world
in all its darkness
and neediness
was her heart heavy
and her throat tight
and her eyes full of unshed tears?
As she put him to her breast
and bore the pain and wonder
of nurturing new life
while others came and went
to marvel at the birth
did her fear for this child
constrict her heart and her lungs?
And as her fear was confirmed
by wise ones
prophesying that this boy child
would pierce her soul
did she smile sweetly
and let others revel in the joy of his birth
while her heart was breaking into pieces?
Did she know that she would travel
from the pain of bearing a child
through the agony of labour
(make no mistake

MIRIAM'S SISTERS, DEBORAH'S DAUGHTERS

God did not have that covered!)
knowing that she must confront
the trauma of a son
who left home early
to be about the business of God
a son who did not return weekly
with his laundry
or looking for a good feed
but who took to the road
and kept on going
because God's business was
a business that involved
itinerant living
hanging out with those labelled losers
upsetting the institutions of the day so much
that ultimately
he would be executed
hung out to dry for fear of insurrection
Mary, the mother of God
endured so much more
than the pain that is simply a part
of mothering a son
that pain of birthing and letting go
that mothers have always borne
And she knew
From the moment she said yes to God
Mary knew
And still she said 'Yes'

13

Leadership as Making Poetry

For women, then, poetry is not a luxury. It is a vital necessity of our existence. It forms the quality of the light within which we predicate our hopes and dreams toward survival and change, first made into language, then into idea, then into more tangible action.
Audre Lorde (1977)

There is a wonderful story in Matthew 15 in which Jesus seems to forget his divinity – or perhaps exploits his divinity! A Canaanite woman comes to ask Jesus for healing for her daughter. When Jesus fails to respond to the woman, she follows and keeps on asking for what she needs. Jesus' disciples plead with him to respond to her so that she will stop bothering them and Jesus responds to his disciples that he was sent only to the lost sheep of the House of Israel.

That seems to hold things up long enough for the woman to catch them up and ask Jesus directly: 'Lord, help me.' To which Jesus responds: 'It is not fair to take the children's food and throw it to the dogs.' Instead of being sent on her way by such a scathing remark, with her tail between her legs (pun intended), the woman daringly responds: 'Even the dogs eat the crumbs that fall from their master's table.' And, just like that, Jesus is confronted with a wit and a will that is a match for his own. He commends the woman's faith, and her daughter is healed.

So often I've heard this incident explained away, to protect Jesus' blushes. In the same way that so much discrimination and bullying and misogyny in the Church is explained away – as just some banter between the boys, all of whom are certainly old enough to know better!

We can do better than that.

We can credit this Canaanite woman with the ability to subvert and disrupt cultural norms. She took Jesus' words and threw them right back at him. And in their little game of catch, Jesus was afforded insight into how to respect someone who could challenge convention and expand notions of the kingdom of God. Jesus saw writ large in this woman, who for a time had become his adversary, someone who refused to submit to injustice and someone who challenged him to do better too. The unnamed Canaanite woman could so easily have traded insults with Jesus. Instead, she chose to use her words to challenge respectfully and so secured her purpose, the healing for her daughter that she so desperately wanted.

When positions become entrenched, it often falls to the women to weave a way through, to cut through stubbornness with words that challenge and move things on.

Women lead by pushing the envelope. That cliché about it being a woman's prerogative to change her mind? That gives license to try new ways or to revert to old and tested ways, all in the name of forging a way that moves beyond the narrow confines of tradition, releases stuck narratives and opens up new possibilities.

It's curious how folk can become entrenched and invested in a model of operating, even a way of being, that no longer fits who they are becoming. Some gentle encouragement to examine closely their core motivations and how their actions enable or impede those can bring insight. And when this introspection is paired with creatively imagining new ways of being, alternative pathways are forged that bring release.

Regular examination of practice helps to identify discrepancies between our espoused and our operant theologies, between what we say we believe and how we live out those beliefs.

It is said that life itself is our best teacher. But we learn best not simply by experience but by reflecting on experience. Establishing the practice of regularly stepping aside accompanied by a skilful practitioner who holds space, not simply for us to report on all that we've accomplished, but for us to reflect on our practice, promotes the potential for learning and growth. And, in our reflecting, there is much to be gained when we can move out of our normal ways of thinking and processing. Part of my portfolio involves facilitating reflective practice with individuals and groups in a variety of professions. When folks feel secure enough to embrace an alternative approach to reflection, to exercise their right brain by working beyond their normal narratives, it is possible to capture insight afforded by an image. Whether that image comes by way of a word-based metaphor or the view outside their window, the shift can be sufficient to provide a changed perspective. And from that new perspective it is possible to envisage a different way forward.

The unnamed Canaanite woman who confronted Jesus disrupted his normal patterns of thinking; she drew Jesus a new picture that threw up new possibilities and enabled Jesus to move his mission into a new realm of welcoming all. By encouraging Jesus to examine how his practice matched his words, she challenged him to not just espouse but to live into a new way of being a Messiah for all.

Seldom will we make that journey on our own. It takes an outsider to accompany us with skilful questions and carefully timed banter. It takes the courage and curiosity of someone who, rather than judge us, will enable us to take a long and loving look at how we live into our calling, will accompany us as we engage in contemplation and seek to live into who we are becoming. It takes an outsider to disrupt our practice and encourage us to contemplate a transformed future in the poetry of leadership.

The Art of Contemplation

Contemplation involves
being willing to go there
to the heart of our practice
being willing to look
and look again
seeing the chasm that yawns in the dark
and being willing to take a step into the darkness
knowing that we come from light
and light awaits
And between those lights
there is a love that holds
so that the dark will not consume
but, rather, be transformed
by courage
and by curiosity
and by the contemplation
of the potential for change

14

Leadership as Finding Our Voice

Word by word, the language of women so often begins with a whisper.
Terry Tempest Williams (2013)

I used to have a cartoon on my pinboard depicting a group of elderly grey-clad men and one woman sitting around a boardroom table. The caption read: 'That's an excellent suggestion, Miss Triggs – now perhaps one of the men would like to make it.'

This image spoke to me of many meetings I'd sat through before I was brave enough to call it out.

Women's suggestions and wise counsel are often underestimated until they are reiterated in a male voice timbre. It took me a long time to learn that, rather than keep silent, it was important to keep on speaking clearly and deliberately.

Scripture also has its share of stories of men refusing to listen to or choosing to disregard women's voices. In Judges 13, an angel appears to an unnamed woman, promising that she will conceive and bear a son. The angel also told her how her son was to be raised as a Nazirite, one of those who among other things drink no wine nor cut their hair. When she told her husband this, he prayed that the angel might appear again and teach them how to raise their son so that he could hear the message for himself. A little later, the angel appeared again to the woman. When she told her husband, he rushed to find the angel, and when he caught up with him asked him what the boy's rule of life would be. Even when the angel told the husband to make sure that his wife did all that had been asked of her, the husband did not take the hint; he insisted the angel stay and feast with them and then he became awestruck when the angel ascended in the flame of the altar. Meanwhile, his wife did everything the angel asked of her and bore a son, whom they named Samson. In time, Samson became one of the judges in Israel. We can speculate on why the angel chose to speak to the mother rather than the father – perhaps the mother was more attuned to the presence of the divine – but it comes as no surprise that the father was sceptical of the message without hearing it for himself.

Many ordinations in our Church take place around Petertide, when we celebrate St Peter's profession of faith. I've always been puzzled that when Peter professed his faith, he was named as the rock on which the Church would be built and was handed the keys of the kingdom. However, when Martha declared her faith, there was no such accolade.

Martha is the woman whom we perhaps associate most readily with her sister Mary. Martha and Mary hosted Jesus at their house. Martha implored Jesus to encourage her sister Mary to help her with all the traditional chores of cultural hospitality. Centuries of men telling the story of that domestic encounter encourages us to surmise that we must take sides, choose Martha or Mary. Choose to be the domestic goddess or the contemplative student. What we see unfolding in that story is a tale of two women who both refused to conform to the cultural norms of the day – Martha by acting as host to the rabbi and Mary by sitting at his feet as a disciple, neither of which would be deemed appropriate. There is an incident recounted in John's Gospel in which Martha makes an astonishing profession of faith by declaring:

> 'Yes, Lord, I believe that you are the Messiah, the Son of God, the one coming into the world.' (John 11.27)

Martha not only believed but understood the words that she uttered, which is more than can be said of Peter.

Mary Magdalene was another woman who encountered Jesus during his ministry and who stuck around until the very end. She was by the Cross as Jesus died. She was one of the women who prepared spices for his burial. And she was the one whom Jesus met in the garden after his Resurrection, a moment not yet tarnished by the unbelief of her male counterparts. When Mary began to proclaim the Resurrection, her message was dismissed as an idle tale by men who wanted to see and hear for themselves.

But in that moment, in the garden, the entire gospel rested on Mary. That's worth a pause. For a time, Mary Magdalene was the first and only witness to the Resurrection. I wonder how long she hugged that delicious predicament to herself? I suspect not nearly long enough. Nevertheless, she had first dibs on a miraculous turn of events.

What a moment that must have been, pregnant with the immensity of potential, cradled in the hands of a woman and birthed in early morning light as she took to her heels to proclaim the good news.

Earlier in the Gospel of Luke, Mary Magdalene is described as a woman 'from whom seven demons had gone out'. She is a woman released to live life to the full. Released to be spontaneous. Released to love. Released to embrace all that she was, to strut her stuff with pride. Released to be fierce and fabulous and to proclaim the Resurrection.

A Woman Possessed

Mary Magdalene
said to be a woman possessed of seven demons
I wonder …
I wonder if those demons were:
A propensity to love with abandon
To display her passions
To be fierce and loyal and persistent
To stay curious
To be spontaneous
To act on her intuition
To be assertive (apparently a deadly sin in women)
In her encounter with Jesus
Mary was freed
to be fully awake to life
and to inhabit wholly
her weird and wondrous calling
to proclaim the Resurrection
He is risen
He is risen indeed
Alleluia!

15

Leadership as Breaking the Mould

There's something so special about a woman who dominates in a man's world. It takes a certain grace, strength, intelligence, fearlessness and the nerve to never take no for an answer.
Rihanna (in conversation)

One year in Holy Week, as I prepared a series of worship encounters, I spent some time with the story of the woman with the alabaster jar, who anointed Jesus' feet and dried them with her hair, a woman often known as Mary of Bethany. Her story is told in all four Gospels, and in each telling the story becomes more about the men around her, the onlookers who claim centre stage. Instead of being a story about this woman's intuition, spontaneity and selfless giving, it becomes a story about Judas, keeper of the purse, or about the righteous Pharisee in whose house the feast was hosted, or even about Jesus' lack of spidey-sense that prevented him from knowing the supposed fallenness of this woman who loved all over him.

This is what happens when women's stories are told by men. They lose something of the substance and the soul of their existence, taking on a one-dimensional hue. Not only were many of these women's stories shared without the women being named, but they were also redacted to fit into a patriarchal narrative.

I've often wondered, in this story of the woman with the alabaster jar, whether some of the men present envied the woman's impetuosity. Did some of those men, constrained by social norms, secretly admire the way she threw herself into demonstrating her love? Did they wish that they could also dispense with cultural expectations and propriety so that they might express freely their response to the disruptive impact that Jesus had on them?

It couldn't have been easy to watch such a display of naked passion. Perhaps some of those present were aroused by the woman's public display of affection and, rather than ponder their arousal, they condemned the object of their awakening? Now there is a familiar story in the realms of purity culture: it's easier to blame the object (and women are always the ones objectified) than to deal with issues of self-control.

In pondering these intriguing possibilities, I am aware of the irony of my distraction as I contemplate how the woman's actions affected those who witnessed her extravagance.

Perhaps that is what such unbridled passion and raw vulnerability evokes: the need to look away for fear that we are confronted with something that touches our soul in ways we would rather not acknowledge. And certainly in our churches, when we recount this story, it will inevitably be toned down to make it more palatable and much less disturbing lest we allow passion to corrupt our worship!

Where do we see modelled the kind of spontaneity that invites us to connect viscerally with the God of love, to have all of our senses awakened – touch, sight, hearing, taste and smell – to be released from the cerebral pattern of response that is often more prevalent in our worship spaces? When our worship is confined to the cerebral it's little wonder that it has slight impact on the rest of our lives. When, however, our senses are awakened by the beauty of music, of liturgy, of movement, of incense, of candles, there is an embodiment that lingers and the sacrament in which we share becomes food for the journey, spilling out into the everyday.

For many years, I was infatuated with Episcopalian worship. I would dip in and out of services, particularly sung Eucharists and evensong. Frequently, I would be moved to tears. Experiencing the raw beauty of the liturgy and receiving the sacrament, often with little interaction with other worshippers – a choice I made – I would be sated for the next wee while, until my next fix. And then life changed. In a new role in ministry, I was no longer the person up front crafting meaningful worship for others. I was free to indulge my senses in worship that encompassed all of me. I luxuriated in the beauty of the liturgy and of the sacrament. I convinced myself that such gluttony was merely temporary, that things would settle down and I would return to worship experiences that were less consuming. I'm still waiting for that to happen. Or, rather, I am grateful that the power of sensual liturgy in which the Blessed Sacrament has a central role still feeds and sustains. One of the ways I have described the experience is by citing my love of playing both violin and cello. I would describe myself as a reasonably proficient violinist, having played since I was eight years old with lots of opportunity to be part of ensembles playing different genres of music, from ceilidh to classical. However, there is something more demanded of me when I take up the cello, an instrument that I didn't start learning until much later in life. There is something about the posture required and the resonance experienced as the strings vibrate that speaks to a different part of my soul.

The woman with the alabaster jar somehow connected her love for Jesus with the Passion that he was about to endure. And she poured her love all over his wounds before they had even been inflicted. How often when we take the bread of the sacrament do we imagine the gaping flesh and jagged wounds of our Lord into which we are invited to put our hands? Or when we drink the cup, are we able to imagine the blood that oozed from the same pores that had been soothed by the oil of a woman's anointing?

And as we turn from the altar to embrace the world again, are we able to connect those sacred offerings with the brokenness in our world today, where bodies are not honoured and where wounds are inflicted with no hope of healing or of care, where life itself is cheap and where governments ply armaments and warfare to protect their power and inflate their economy with scant regard for the real collateral of their cruel games? A world in which those who speak truth or practice love are vilified to provide a distraction from nefarious acts?

The selfless act of a woman anointing her beloved before death is one perpetuated throughout the world as wars are fought in places near and far, and as lives are traded for pieces of empire that signal wealth and power, and as authoritarian control mitigates against justice. And still today, we avert our eyes rather than confront the evils of supremacy that continue to perpetrate violence and subjugate love.

The woman with the alabaster jar chose to smash to pieces convention and propriety so that love might be wholly visible. Powerful leadership entails embracing vulnerability with all of our senses until the sheer discomfort forces us to act with fierce love.

Recovering Her Story

It's all about her
The woman who saw the man she loved with a passion
hell bent on riling the authorities
who were already out to get him
Knowing she couldn't save his skin
she anointed it
pouring out her precious ointment
allowing it to soak all the way in
soothing, healing
pouring out her emotion
brimful of love
unadulterated, unfiltered love
that could no longer be contained
Broken open
like the alabaster jar
she worshipped her beloved
with all that she had
In days or years to come
did she drift back to that moment
when she allowed her heart
to rule her head
and was she comforted in the knowledge
that she didn't hold back
but gave him all her loving?

16

Leadership as Fostering Wellbeing

To be fully seen is a rare and transformative gift.
Mirabai Starr (2019)

When I hear organizations and agencies speak about wellbeing, I am immediately drawn to the Gospel story in John 4 of the woman at the well. Being at the well provided women with an opportunity not only to draw water for their households but to catch up with the stories and the wisdom of the day. To share with and to learn from one another. The woman, who is unnamed in John 4 but named in Eastern Orthodox traditions as Photini, bearer of light, finds herself alone with Jesus. Based on her testimony, it is not long before the rest of the community pitches up at the well to encounter Jesus for themselves and to discover the source of living water.

I imagine those watering places as places where women gathered in community, and bore witness to one another's stories, stories of trials and tribulations, of joys and sorrows, where they learned from one another and where they challenged one another. Rather than being 'talked over' as is often the way in boardroom or committee discussions, women have the propensity to hold space for one another to be fully seen and heard.

As I accompanied congregational leaders through transition, one of the most transformative elements was the creation of a non-competitive environment. This was partly achieved by the acknowledgement that we were embarking on uncharted territory, where current maps, such as they were, did not serve well in the prevalent topography. It was also the conscious creation of relationships based not so much on experience and expertise but on charting a way forward together, taking cognisance of the many different contexts in which we worked. In our vulnerability we were able to support one another by gathering around the well to share our stories and, in being heard, to harness courage to take the next steps on our various journeys. Listening becomes sacred work when we are willing to be involved in communal discernment.

Much of the work of reflective practice in diverse workspaces seeks to facilitate such a space for individuals and for groups, a space in which each participates not out of strength but out of weakness, offering their questioning as a resource for reflection.

Nancy Kline describes how the quality of listening we are offered affects the quality of thinking we are able to do (2002). When we know we will not be interrupted, we can take time to formulate our thoughts, to try out ideas that are developing and to know ourselves heard. She describes three ways of listening:

- Listening to interrupt, in which we are constantly thinking about how we might contribute to the conversation and what we might say next. Most conversations operate on this level of interaction.

- Listening to understand, in which we seek clarification on what is being said. While this can be a helpful and enlightening conversation for the listener, it exists at the level of information exchange and does not contribute to the real work of sense making for the speaker.
- Listening to ignite, in which the conversation flows around the energy of the speaker, facilitating deeper insight and awareness.

Wellbeing consists in being fully seen and heard, valued as co-contributors in spaces of learning and of transformation.

> Then the woman left her water jar and went back to the city. She said to the people, 'Come and see a man who told me everything I have ever done! He cannot be the Messiah, can he?' They left the city and were on their way to him. (John 4.28–30)

Resonance

Found in the deep bass notes
achieved by laying the fingers
firmly on the strings
and letting the bow dig in
Found, too, in the sweet, high pitch of a harmonic
called forth by the lightest touch
that gently coaxes out a beauty
that may be lost
to those whose hearing is dulled
by all the background noise
or the tiredness of tuning in
The initial sound
is but a prelude
to the depth that lingers
beneath the surface
or the oscillation
that continues to disturb
long after the sound waves
have stilled
We who listen
are called to go there
Invited to stay
with the ripple that continues
when the movement has stopped

17

Leadership as Collaboration

Our deepest fear is not that we are inadequate. Our deepest fear is that we are powerful beyond measure.
Marianne Williamson (2015)

I urge Euodia and I urge Syntyche to be of the same mind in the Lord.
Philippians 4.2

This text from Philippians has often been used to suggest that there was some dispute between these two women leaders in the early Church. I wonder. What if it was instead an encouragement to them to stay strong amid the persecution that was rife, an acknowledgement of the strength that between them they might access? Or even a rallying call for them to keep on doing as they are doing?

Throughout the accounts of early Church life as recounted in the Acts of the Apostles and in various Epistles, numerous named and unnamed women hold central roles in Church and community life. In Romans 16 alone nine women are mentioned, seven by name: Phoebe, Priscilla, Mary, Junia, Tryphaena, Tryphosa, Rufus' mother, Julia and Nereus' sister.

The women we find are providing care, hospitality, funding,

MIRIAM'S SISTERS, DEBORAH'S DAUGHTERS

clothing, attending to body, mind and soul in everyday life. These are the women who, sometimes literally, were stitching the Church together. The roles and tasks of the plethora of women speak volumes about their cooperation and creativity, about their ability to network, about their grasp of the political and social climates that prevailed, and the myriad ways they endeavoured to create community where the gospel was not simply taught and preached but lived out.

Much has been uncovered, documented and shared in recent years about the life of trees and how they are intricately connected by vast underground systems of mycelium. These fungal roots forge connections, share nutrients and signal when all is not well. Ecologist Suzanne Simard (2022) has also identified Mother Trees that, because of their age and depths of their root systems, can nurture and sustain other trees in the network, even responding to distress signals when required. I imagine the women in the early Church in a similar vein, possessing a vast store of wisdom and ways of connecting to further the spread of the gospel, providing nurture and sustenance as they went.

We have a favourite island in the Scottish Inner Hebrides that we've holidayed on for over 40 years. Usually arriving on a Friday, we would have a quiet couple of days before attending church on the Sunday. It's there at church that we would meet friends and acquaintances and connect more fully with island life. We'd hear how folks were faring, catch up on the latest news, arrange coffee meet-ups and lunch dates for the rest of our stay and, in the midst of all this, we would break bread together. When the Apostles entered a new city on their travels, they often went to the river where they knew they would find some women praying. There, they knew, they could make the connections they needed for their ongoing mission.

LEADERSHIP AS COLLABORATION

> On the sabbath day we went outside the gate by the river, where we supposed there was a place of prayer; and we sat down and spoke to the women who had gathered there. (Acts 16.13)

The details are scant and often fleeting but here are a few snapshots that have emerged of some of the women involved in this intricate worldwide web.

Phoebe most probably took Paul's letter to the Romans not simply as a courier but as one who could share its contents and answer questions.

Priscilla with her husband Aquila accompanied Paul for part of his missionary journeys and, on reaching Ephesus, stayed to minister in the church there. They were instrumental in Apollos' Christian formation.

Junia, though we hear little about her, is described as an 'outstanding apostle', quite the accolade, and it is recorded that she spent time in prison with Paul (Rom. 16.7).

Tabitha, whom Peter raised from the dead, 'was devoted to good works and acts of charity' (Acts 9.36). As her friends mourned her passing, they showed Peter examples of her work in making garments.

Lydia, 'a dealer in purple cloth' (Acts 11.14), was one of the women that Paul and Silas encountered in Philippi. She was one of the women who went down to the river to pray, a first port of call for the Apostles when they entered unknown territory and wanted to find some people of peace, as we saw earlier.

Rhoda served as a maid at the house of Mary who was John Mark's mother. One night, as they prayed for Peter's release from prison, Peter showed up at the gate. Rhoda was so astonished at seeing him that she left him standing there and ran to tell the others.

Lois was grandmother of Timothy and Eunice was his mother. When Paul writes to Timothy, he commends the faith of the two women.

We also hear of Damaris, Chloe, Claudia, Apphia, Persis and Julia, a whole plethora of names of women who courageously collaborated in ministry, undertaking tasks large and small to facilitate growth in the early Church.

I imagine these named and the unnamed women as an unstoppable force for good, networking across the ancient world, over land and sea, propellants of the gospel locally and globally. I marvel at the scale of their industry and the reach of their ministrations, their attention to every detail, feeding, clothing, teaching, carrying, healing, nurturing; the sheer logistics are mind-boggling. And I like to think that those who made garments in this vast endeavour sewed pockets in women's dresses, leaving room for much sedition.

Women with Pockets in Their Dresses

It is said
that putting pockets in women's dresses
will lead to sedition
please count me in
I want pockets in all my dresses
Big pockets for my latest project
be it crocheted hearts or angels
or knitted socks or fingerless gloves
Small pockets for badges and buttons
that declare my mood on any given day
And normal-sized pockets for a book of poems
or my multi-tool that will unscrew a battery cover
or smash a window when I need to escape
And of course there will be a pocket for my phone
on which all the seditious material will be stored
with which I can garner support and promote a protest
or invoke a gathering of friends
Even wedding dresses today
are carefully crafted with pockets
so that brides can start as they mean to continue
with sedition on their minds
The worldwide web of women begins
with sewing pockets in women's dresses

18

Navigating by Old Landmarks

A few years ago, three tower blocks were demolished in my hometown. They were brought down in a controlled explosion in the early hours of the morning. Just over 40 years ago, my grandparents and their neighbours had been among the first residents of those brand new homes. At the time, they were the latest in local authority housing provision, having central heating, drying areas and shiny new lifts that worked really well – in the beginning. Being compulsorily moved out of the homes they had known, in buildings that were crumbling around them and long overdue for demolition, my grandparents and their neighbours were well pleased with their new homes. Forty years doesn't seem like a very long shelf life but already their home and two other 15-storey tower blocks have been razed to the ground. But that doesn't stop local residents giving directions by using the tower blocks that are no longer there as a point of reference: 'Turn left just where the high flats used to be.' The ground has been reclaimed by landscapers and there is little trace of what used to be a thriving community of industrious people.

MIRIAM'S SISTERS, DEBORAH'S DAUGHTERS

That strikes me as a metaphor for much of our faith structures that we navigate by reference to missing landmarks. Buildings have been demolished. People have moved on. Landscapers have transformed the area. And we are still trying to navigate using old maps that no longer make any sense, using tools of leadership that no longer have any purchase.

Some are busy drawing up new maps that can't possibly keep up with the pace of change. Others are frantically designing sophisticated new tools that are heavy and unwieldy and take months of training to use.

Leadership that looks like Deborah gathering stories under a tree, or Miriam leading the women in dance, Shiphrah and Puah delivering new life, Photini at the well sharing wisdom, Vashti saying 'No', Rizpah keeping vigil, Mary singing her song of revolt, all subverting the straitjackets of conformity and order, freeing the wildness of God to be unleashed on a world where provisional is the best we can hope for and where the invitation is: 'Try it and see.' Give the spirit of God space to meander where she will, follow in her wake and be caught up in the slipstream that crosses the threshold of God's love and abundance, treading in the footsteps of our sisters who are singing us all the way home. Let me tread with you through the broken waters that signal new life.

Epitaph

I want my epitaph to read
'She stood on the shoulders of strong women
and held the door open for others'
Too often the soundscape
is a door slamming shut
its echo through the hallway
signalling there's no welcome here
or the tinkling sound of tiny glass shards
being replaced to reinforce the glass ceiling
in a bid to prevent any further breach
I dream of wandering hallowed hallways
where the doors are propped open
inviting all to enter
bringing their curiosity
and their difference
and where the floors are carpeted
with myriad hues of stained glass
whose sharp edges have become worn and smooth
and are now fashioned into
a colourful kaleidoscope
that shakes up the layers
that have gathered over the years
and rearranges them
as a celebration
of all who have gone before
and of all who have yet to find
the cacophony
of story making together
that celebrates how women lead the way

References and Further Reading

Atwood, M., 1990, 'Margaret Atwood, The Art of Fiction No. 121', *The Paris Review*, 117, at https://www.theparisreview.org/interviews/2262/the-art-of-fiction-no-121-margaret-atwood (accessed 17.10.24).

Bauby, J.-D., 1997, *The Diving Bell and the Butterfly*, Harper Collins.

Gafney, W., 2008, *Daughters of Miriam: Women Prophets in Ancient Israel*, Fortress Press.

Gafney, Wil P., 2012, *Womanists Wading in the Word*, at https://www.wilgafney.com/2012/03/25/lessons-from-the-prophet-miriam-when-you-mess-up-step-up (accessed 17.10.24).

Gorman, A., 2022, 'Won't You be My Sister', in *Little People, Big Dreams*, Frances Lincoln Children's Books.

Greer, G., 2020, *The Female Eunuch*, Harper.

Joukhadar, J., 2019, *The Map of Salt and Stars*, Weidenfeld & Nicolson.

Kline, N., 2002, *Time to Think*, Cassell.

Koluder, A., 2021, Information and Communication Technology Training, Emphasys Centre, at https://emphasyscentre.com/2021/03/16/%F0%9F%92%AD-a-refugee-is-someone-who-survived-and-who-can-create-the-future-amela-koluder (accessed 17.10.24).

Lizzo, 2022, at https://people.com/health/lizzo-most-empowering-quotes/ (accessed 17.10.24).

Lorde, A., 1977, 'Poetry is Not a Luxury', essay, at https://making

learning.wordpress.com/wp-content/uploads/2014/01/poetry-is-not-a-luxury-audre-lorde.pdf (accessed 17.10.24).

Maines, N., 2022, The Chicks, at https://www.thechicks.com (accessed 17.10.24).

Oliver, M., 2010, *Evidence: Poems*, Beacon Press.

Ruttenberg, D., 2024, *Life is a Sacred Text*, Whose Truth at https://www.lifeisasacredtext.com (accessed 17.10.24).

Shetterly, M. L., 2016, *Hidden Figures*, William Morrow.

Simard, S., 2022, *Finding the Mother Tree*, Penguin.

Starr, M., 2019, *Wild Mercy: Living the Fierce and Tender Wisdom of the Women Mystics*, Sounds True Adult.

Williams, T. T., 2013, *When Women were Birds: Fifty Four Variations on Voice*, Picador.

Williamson, M., 2015, *A Return to Love: Reflections on the Principles of a Course in Miracles*, Harper Thorsons.

www.ingramcontent.com/pod-product-compliance
Lightning Source LLC
Chambersburg PA
CBHW060612080526
44585CB00013B/791